Lecture Notes in Bioinformatics　　　13060

Subseries of Lecture Notes in Computer Science

More information about this subseries at https://link.springer.com/bookseries/5381

George Bebis · Terry Gaasterland ·
Mamoru Kato · Mohammad Kohandel ·
Kathleen Wilkie (Eds.)

Mathematical and Computational Oncology

Third International Symposium, ISMCO 2021
Virtual Event, October 11–13, 2021
Proceedings

 Springer

Editors
George Bebis
University of Nevada Reno
Reno, NV, USA

Mamoru Kato
National Cancer Center Japan
Tokyo, Japan

Kathleen Wilkie
Ryerson University
Toronto, ON, Canada

Terry Gaasterland
Scripps Genome Center,
Scripps Institution of Oceanography
UC San Diego
San Diego, USA

Mohammad Kohandel
Department of Applied Mathematics
University of Waterloo
Waterloo, ON, Canada

ISSN 0302-9743   ISSN 1611-3349   (electronic)
Lecture Notes in Bioinformatics
ISBN 978-3-030-91240-6   ISBN 978-3-030-91241-3   (eBook)
https://doi.org/10.1007/978-3-030-91241-3

LNCS Sublibrary: SL8 – Bioinformatics

This Springer imprint is published by the registered company Springer Nature Switzerland AG
The registered company address is: Gewerbestrasse 11, 6330 Cham, Switzerland

Preface

It is with great pleasure that we welcome you to the proceedings of the 3rd International Symposium on Mathematical and Computational Oncology (ISMCO 2021), which was held virtually (October 11–13, 2021).

Despite significant advances in the understanding of the principal mechanisms leading to various cancer types, less progress has been made toward developing patient-specific treatments. Advanced mathematical and computational models could play a significant role in examining the most effective patient-specific therapies. The purpose of ISMCO is to provide a common interdisciplinary forum for mathematicians, scientists, engineers and clinical oncologists throughout the world to present and discuss their latest research findings, ideas, developments and applications in mathematical and computational oncology. In particular, ISMCO aspires to forge stronger relationships among researchers in a variety of disciplines, including mathematics, physical sciences, computer science, data science, engineering and oncology, with the goal of developing new insights into the pathogenesis and treatment of malignancies.

The program includes 6 keynote presentations, 6 oral sessions, 1 panel discussion, and 2 tutorials. ISMCO 2021 received 20 submissions, from which we accepted 16 submissions for oral presentation. This LNBI volume includes only the full and short papers accepted for presentation. All abstracts that were accepted for presentation appear in an online volume, which was published by Frontiers (a link is provided on the ISMCO website).

All submissions were reviewed with an emphasis on the potential to contribute to the state of the art in the field. Selection criteria included accuracy and originality of ideas, clarity and significance of results, and presentation quality. The review process was quite rigorous, involving at least three independent double-blind reviews, followed by several days of discussion. During the discussion period, we tried to correct anomalies and errors that might have existed in the initial reviews. Despite our efforts, we recognize that some papers worthy of inclusion may not be in the program. We offer our sincere apologies to authors whose contributions may have been overlooked.

Many contributed to the success of ISMCO 2021. First and foremost, we are grateful to the Steering, Organizing, and Program Committees; they strongly welcomed, supported, and promoted the organization of this new meeting. Second, we are deeply indebted to the keynote speakers who warmly accepted our invitation to talk at ISMCO 2021; their reputation in mathematical and computational oncology added significant value and excitement to the meeting. Next, we wish to thank the authors who submitted their work to ISMCO 2021 and the reviewers who helped us to evaluate the quality of the submissions. It was because of their contributions that we succeeded in putting together a high-quality technical program. Finally, we would like to express our appreciation to Springer, Frontiers and the International Society for Computational Biology (ISCB) for supporting ISMCO 2021.

We sincerely hope that despite the difficulties due to the pandemic, ISMCO 2021 offered participants opportunities for professional growth. We look forward to many more successful meetings in mathematical and computational oncology.

October 2021

George Bebis
Terry Gaasterland
Mamoru Kato
Mohammad Kohandel
Kathleen Wilkie

Organization

Steering Committee

Anastasiadis Panagiotis	Mayo Clinic
Bebis George (Chair)	University of Nevada, Reno
Jackson Trachette	University of Michigan
Levy Doron	University of Maryland, College Park
Rockne Russell	City of Hope
Vasmatzis George	Mayo Clinic
Yankeelov Thomas	University of Texas, Austin

Program Chairs

Gaasterland Terry	University of California, San Diego
Kato Mamoru	National Cancer Center Japan
Kohandel Mohammad	University of Waterloo
Wilkie Kathleen	Ryerson University

Publicity Chair

Loss Leandro	QuantaVerse

Tutorials and Special Tracks Chairs

Bebis George	University of Nevada, Reno
Nguyen Tin	University of Nevada, Reno

Awards

Cho Heyrim	University of California, Riverside
Gevertz Jana	The College of New Jersey

Web Master

Isayas Berhe Adhanom	University of Nevada, Reno

Discussion Panel

Bringing Mathematical Methods to the Broader Oncology Community

Moderator

Deslattes Mays Anne	Science and Technology Consulting, LLC

Panelists

Soheil Meshinchi	Fred Hutchinson Cancer Center
Ching Lau	The Jackson Laboratory
Adam Resnick	The Children's Hospital of Philadelphia
Lincoln Stein	Ontario Institute for Cancer Research
Jinghui Zhang	St. Jude Children's Research Hospital

Tutorials

(1) Current methods and open challenges for structural modeling in cancer immunotherapy - 3rd Edition

Instructors:

Antunes Dinler	Rice University, USA
Fonseca Andre	University of Houston, USA
Hall-Swan Sarah	Rice University, USA
Lydia Kavraki	Rice University, USA
Rigo Mauricio	Pontifical Catholic University of Rio Grande do Sul, Brazil

(2) How can (experimental) data go on tumor growth models?

Instructors:

Ernesto Lima	The University of Texas at Austin, USA
Emanuelle A. Paixao	National Laboratory of Scientific Computing (LNCC), Brazil

Program Committee

Frederick Adler	University of Utah, USA
Pankaj Agarwal	BioInfi
M. Ali Al-Radhawi	Northeastern University, USA
Max Alekseyev	George Washington University, USA
Sanjay Aneja	Yale School of Medicine, USA
Igor Balaz	University of Novi Sad, Serbia
Matteo Barberis	University of Surrey, UK
George Bebis	University of Nevada, USA
Takis Benos	University of Pittsburgh, USA
Debswapna Bhattacharya	Auburn University, USA
Francesco Bianconi	Università degli Studi di Perugia, Italy
Ivana Bozic	University of Washington, USA
Ernesto Augusto Bueno Da Fonseca Lima	The University of Texas at Austin, USA

Anton Buzdin   Omicsway Corp., USA
Raffaele Calogero   University of Torino, Italy
Young-Hwan Chang   Oregon Health and Science University, USA
Aristotelis Chatziioannou   National Hellenic Research Foundation, Greece
Ken Chen   MD Anderson Cancer Center, USA
Luonan Chen   Chinese Academy of Sciences, China
Nicholas Chia   Mayo Clinic, USA
Juan Carlos Chimal   Centro de Investigación en Computación del IPN, Mexico
Heyrim Cho   University of California, Riverside, USA
Jean Clairambault   Inria, France
Francois Cornelis   Sorbonne University, France
Marilisa Cortesi   University of Bologna, Italy
James Costello   University of Colorado, Anschutz Medical Campus, USA
Paul-Henry Cournede   CentraleSupélec, France
Morgan Craig   University of Montreal, Canada
Kit Curtius   University of California, San Diego, USA
Sylvain Cussat-Blanc   University of Toulouse, France
Francesca Demichelis   University of Trento, Italy
Anne Deslattes Mays   Science and Technology Consulting, LLC, USA
Mohammed El-Kebir   University of Illinois at Urbana-Champaign, USA
Peter Elkin   Ontolimatics, USA
Dalit Engelhardt   Dana-Farber Cancer Institute, USA
Terry Gaasterland   University of California San Diego, USA
Andrew Gentles   Stanford University, USA
Jana Gevertz   The College of New Jersey, USA
Preetam Ghosh   Virginia Commonwealth University, USA
James Glazier   Indiana University Bloomington, USA
Jeremy Goecks   Oregon Health and Science University, USA
David Robert Grimes   Dublin City University, Ireland
Wei Gu   University of Luxembourg and ELIXIR-LU, Luxembourg
Hiroshi Haeno   National Cancer Center, Japan
Michael Hallett   Concordia University, Canada
Arif Harmanci   University of Texas Health Sciences Center, USA
Leonard Harris   University of Arkansas, USA
Andrea Hawkins-Daarud   Mayo Clinic, USA
Harry Hochheiser   University of Pittsburgh, USA
Sharon Hori   Stanford University, USA
David Hormuth   The University of Texas at Austin
Florence Hubert   Aix-Marseille Université, France
Trachette Jackson   University of Michigan, USA
Rajkumar Jain   Indore Institute of Science and Technology, India
Xiaowei Jiang   Xi'an Jiaotong-Liverpool University, China
Juan Jiménez-Sánchez   University of Castilla-La Mancha, Spain

Martin Pirkl	ETH Zurich, Switzerland
Angela Pisco	Chan Zuckerberg Biohub, USA
Fateme Pourhasanzade	University of Bergen, Norway
Justin Pritchard	Pennsylvania State University, USA
Natasa Przulj	University College London, UK
Bernhard Renard	Robert Koch Institute, Germany
Mauricio M. Rigo	Rice University, USA
Isidore Rigoutsos	IBM Thomas J Watson Research Center, USA
Maria Rodriguez Martinez	IBM, Zurich Research Laboratory, Switzerland
Anguraj Sadanandam	Institute of Cancer Research, UK
Venkata Pardhasaradhi Satagopam	University of Luxembourg and ELIXIR-LU, Luxembourg
Fabien Scalzo	University of California, Los Angeles, USA
Martin H. Schaefer	Centre for Genomic Regulation, Spain
Alfred Schissler	Lussier Lab, USA
Alexander Schoenhuth	Centrum Wiskunde & Informatica, The Netherlands
Russell Schwartz	Carnegie Mellon University, USA
Roland Schwarz	Max Delbrueck Center for Molecular Medicine, Germany
Yang Shen	Texas A&M University, USA
Eduardo Sontag	Northeastern University, USA
Katerina Stankova	Maastricht University, The Netherlands
Angelique Stephanou	TIMC-IMAG - CNRS, France
Rick Stevens	University of Chicago and Argonne National Laboratory, USA
Peter Sykacek	University of Natural Resources and Life Sciences, Austria
Ewa Szczurek	University of Warsaw, Poland
Johannes Textor	Radboudumc, The Netherlands
Xiaojun Tian	Arizona State University, USA
Dumitru Trucu	University of Dundee, UK
Tamir Tuller	Tel Aviv University, Israel
Daniela Ushizima	Lawrence Berkeley National Laboratory, USA
Vahideh Vakil	Rutgers University, USA
George Vasmatzis	Mayo Clinic, USA
Yannick Viossat	Université Paris-Dauphine, France
Mark Wass	University of Kent, UK
Kathleen Wilkie	Ryerson University, Canada
Yanji Xu	NIH, USA
Rui Yamaguchi	Aichi Cancer Center Research Institute, Japan
Bo Yuan	Harvard University, USA
Meirav Zehavi	Ben-Gurion University, Israel
Alex Zelikovsky	Georgia State University, USA

Keynote Talks

Precision Oncology via the Tumor Transcriptome

Eytan Ruppin

CDSL, NCI, NIH, USA

Abstract. Precision oncology has made significant advances, mainly by targeting actionable mutations and fusion events involving cancer driver genes. Aiming to expand treatment opportunities, recent studies have begun to explore the utility of tumor transcriptome to guide patient treatment. I will introduce a new approach, termed SELECT, which harnesses genetic interactions to successfully predict patient response to cancer therapy from the tumor transcriptome. SELECT is tested on a broad collection of 35 published targeted and immunotherapy clinical trials from 10 different cancer types. It is predictive of patients' response in 80% of these clinical trials and in the recent multi-arm WINTHER trial. In summary, we report the first systematic, transcriptomics-based approach that is predictive across many targeted and immune therapies. The predictive signatures and the code are made publicly available for academic use, laying a basis for future prospective clinical studies. As time permits, I will provide a brief overview of MadHitter, a new approach for guiding precision cancer therapy based on single cell tumor transcriptomics.

Population Genomic Approaches for Molecular Biomarker Discovery in Clinical Oncology

Elli Papaemmanuil

Memorial Sloan Kettering Cancer Center, USA

Abstract. Recent characterization of the genes recurrently mutated in cancer have led to the routine implementation of tumor profiling at diagnosis with the expectation to diagnose and treat patients according to their unique molecular profile - the vision of precision medicine. However, development of molecularly guided clinical decision support tools warrants the delivery of evidence based, data driven, comprehensive models that extend beyond single markers. In my talk I will discuss critical considerations for biomarker characterization, statistical model development, and clinical decision support tool development for clinical adoption.

Speaker Bio-Sketch: Dr. Papaemmanuil got her BSc and MSci in Human Molecular Genetics with Honors at the University of Glasgow and her PhD in Human population genetics at the Institute of Cancer Research in London. She performed her postdoctoral studies at the Wellcome Trust Sanger Center and joined the University of Cambridge as faculty, prior to moving to the Memorial Sloan Kettering Cancer Center. Dr. Papaemmanuil has employed genome profiling methodologies to study the role of acquired mutations in cancer development and how these determine clinical phenotype and response to therapy. More recently she has established high-throughput laboratory profiling approaches and developed statistical modelling methodologies that integrate clinical and molecular parameters to inform patient tailored disease classification and clinical decision support (prognosis and treatment decisions). Her main research motivation is to develop research that helps translate recent cancer genome discoveries into clinical practice. Her current research spans, bioinformatic and algorithmic platform development, biomarker discovery and validation and experimental models of disease biology. Additionally, Dr. Papaemmanuil has a strong interest to understand the effects of treatment in disease progression and genetic drivers of treatment response. Dr. Papaemmanuil leads the Pediatrics Precision medicine initiative for MSK Kids, which sets out to evaluate, validate and deliver a clinical prototype for integrative whole genome and whole transcriptome sequencing analyses to understand mechanisms of disease biology and guide treatment strategies in pediatric cancers.

Three Problems in Mathematical Oncology

Paul K. Newton

Viterbi School of Engineering and Ellison Institute for Transformative Medicine,
University of Southern California, USA

Abstract. I will introduce three problems in mathematical oncology all of which
involve nonlinear dynamics and control theory. First, I will describe our work
using Markov chain models to forecast metastatic progression. The models treat
progression as a (weighted) random walk on a directed graph whose nodes are
tumor locations, with transition probabilities obtained through historical autopsy
date (untreated progression) and longitudinal data (treated) from Memorial
Sloan Kettering and MD Anderson Cancer Centers. Then, I will describe our
models (both deterministic and stochastic) that use evolutionary game theory
(replicator dynamics/Moran processes with prisoner's dilemma payoff matrix) to
design multi-drug adaptive chemotherapy schedules to mitigate
chemo-resistance by suppressing 'competitive release' of resistant cell populations. The models highlight the advantages of antagonistic drug interactions
(over synergistic ones) in shaping the fitness landscape of co-evolving populations. Finally, I will describe our work on developing optimal control
schedules (based on Pontryagin's maximum principle) that maximize coopera-
tion for prisoner's dilemma replicator dynamical systems.

Towards Optimizing Therapy on a Patient Specific Basis via Imaging-Based Mathematical Modeling

Tom Yankeelov

Oden Institute for Computational Engineering and Sciences, Livestrong Cancer Institutes, Departments of Biomedical Engineering, Diagnostic Medicine, Oncology, The University of Texas at Austin, USA

Abstract. The ability to accurately predict the response of tumors to therapy, and then use this information to optimize treatment on an individual patient basis, would dramatically transform oncology. In an attempt to move in this direction, we have developed a clinical-mathematical framework that integrates quantitative magnetic resonance imaging (MRI) data into mechanism-based mathematical models to predict the response of locally advanced breast cancer to neoadjuvant therapy. We will present our recent efforts on this topic and then discuss how these methods can be extended to enable patient-specific simulations of treatment response to a range of therapeutic regimens, thereby providing a pathway for optimizing therapy on a patient-specific basis.

Barrett's Esophagus: Efficient Design of Multiscale Simulations for Surveillance And Treatment

Georg Luebeck

Fred Hutchinson Cancer Research Center, USA

Abstract. Barrett's Esophagus (BE), a metaplastic tissue alteration associated with gastroesophageal reflux, predisposes to esophageal adenocarcinoma (EAC). Endoscopic screening of patients with persistent symptomatic reflux aims to identify patients with BE at risk of progressing to cancer. Such patients are recommended to undergo follow-up examinations for dysplasia or small cancers in the earliest stages. This is useful because the prognosis for EAC detected at an early stage is dramatically better than for advanced stages that are mostly lethal. Thus, endoscopic surveillance of BE, in which multiple biopsies are routinely examined for preneoplastic changes and/or early neoplastic lesions, will increase patient survival compared with patients diagnosed with EAC without prior BE surveillance. However, over-diagnosis is a major concern because the annual rate of progression from BE to EAC is less than 1% overall but depends on age, gender, race/ethnicity, BE segment length, history of gastroesophageal reflux and other life-style factors. Multiscale models that include these factors have been developed but suffer computational bottlenecks and are technically demanding. In this talk I will discuss how mathematical insights and multitype branching process theory can be used to significantly speed up simulations to assess and evaluate various screening modalities in a large number of individuals.

Integrative Methods for Deciphering Cancer Networks

Mona Singh

Princeton University, USA

Abstract. Networks of molecular interactions underlie virtually all functions executed within a cell. Networks thus provide a powerful foundation within which to interpret a wide range of rapidly accumulating biological data. In this talk, I will present formulations and algorithms that leverage the structure and function of biological networks in order to analyze cancer genomes and discover cancer-relevant genes. This is a difficult task, as numerous somatic mutations are typically observed in each cancer genome, only a subset of which are cancer-relevant, and very few genes are found to be somatically mutated across large numbers of individuals. I will introduce a framework that can rapidly integrate multiple sources of information about molecular functionality in order to discover key interactions within a network that tend to be disrupted in cancers. Crucially, our approach is based on analytical calculations that obviate the need to perform time-prohibitive permutation-based significance tests. Next, I will describe algorithms that consider both prior and newly collected data within a network context in order to uncover cancer-relevant subnetworks. Overall, our work showcases the versatility and power of a network viewpoint in advancing biomedical discovery.

Contents

Contents

Statistical and Machine Learning Methods for Cancer Research

Image Classification of Skin Cancer: Using Deep Learning as a Tool for Skin Self-examinations

Kristen Anderson[1,2] (iD) and Sharon S. Hori[1,3,4](✉) (iD)

[1] Department of Radiology, Stanford University School of Medicine, Stanford, CA, USA
shori@stanford.edu
[2] Canary Cancer Research Education Summer Training (CREST) Program, Stanford University School of Medicine, Stanford, CA, USA
[3] Canary Center at Stanford, Stanford University School of Medicine, Stanford, CA, USA
[4] Molecular Imaging Program at Stanford, Stanford University School of Medicine, Stanford, CA, USA

Abstract. Skin cancer is the most common cancer in the United States, and studies indicate that its incidence is rapidly increasing. Regular skin self-examinations enable early cancer detection and intervention and are recommended in addition to clinician-based examinations. However, some patients struggle to identify high-risk skin lesions due to the presence of an overwhelming number of lesions, as well as the subtlety of changes to their skin over time. Artificial intelligence (AI) offers an at-home solution to filter low-risk lesions from a patient's self-examination, thereby reducing the number of lesions requiring routine monitoring. This allows patients to triage lesions during their self-examinations, focus primarily on monitoring high-risk lesions between clinical visits, and become aware when clinical inspection or follow-up is needed. We used the HAM10000 skin cancer dataset from Harvard Dataverse to develop deep-learning algorithms that aid in skin self-examination. ResNet-50, DenseNet-121, and VGG-16 models were used to distinguish low-risk lesions (melanocytic nevi, dermatofibroma, and benign keratosis-like lesions) from high-risk lesions (melanoma, basal cell carcinoma, actinic keratoses, and vascular lesions). Each model generated a prediction score ranging from 0 to 1, where 1 was classified as high-risk and 0 was classified as low-risk. To minimize the number of high-risk lesions classified as low-risk, a threshold of 0.01 was selected for differentiating classes, ensuring only predictions with high-confidence remained in the low-risk bracket. Once the classification threshold between low-risk and high-risk was adjusted, the VGG-16 algorithm removed 50.7% of images from self-examination workload with a precision value in the low-risk category of 0.98 and a recall value of 0.96 for high-risk lesions. The VGG-16 neural net outperformed alternative ResNet-50 and DenseNet-121 models. This work has the potential to make the task of skin self-examination more manageable for patients by identifying which suspicious lesions require follow-up consultation with a clinician.

Keywords: Skin cancer · Melanoma · Deep learning · Convolutional neural network · Dermatology

© Springer Nature Switzerland AG 2021
G. Bebis et al. (Eds.): ISMCO 2021, LNBI 13060, pp. 3–8, 2021.
https://doi.org/10.1007/978-3-030-91241-3_1

1   Introduction

Skin cancer is the most common cancer in the United States, and studies indicate that its incidence is rapidly increasing [1–3]. Melanoma constitutes only 2% of skin cancers but results in the most malignancies and skin cancer mortalities [2, 4]. A diagnosis of melanoma increases a patient's risk for secondary melanomas and recurrence of the primary melanoma [5]. Regular skin self-examinations enable early cancer detection and intervention; they are recommended in addition to clinician-based examinations [6]. However, some patients struggle to identify high-risk skin lesions due to the presence of an overwhelming number of lesions, as well as the subtlety of changes to their skin over time [6].

Research using artificial intelligence (AI) to diagnose skin lesions has progressed with a focus on stand-alone AI diagnostics [7, 8]. Yet, the utility of AI in self-examinations relies on patient receptiveness. A study conducted on the patient perspective of AI in skin cancer found that 59% of 298 surveyed respondents were unamenable to using AI as a stand-alone system, while 94% of participants favored the use of AI as an assistant [9]. To balance these concerns, patients should have access to an accurate skin self-examination strategy that prioritizes patient autonomy, AI efficiency, and clinician feedback.

We propose that AI offers an at-home solution to filter low-risk lesions from a patient's self-examination, reducing the number of lesions requiring routine monitoring. Patients may triage lesions during their self-examinations, focus primarily on monitoring high-risk lesions between clinical visits, and become aware when clinical inspection or follow-up is needed. In this study, we aimed to make skin self-examinations more efficient in between regular clinical visits, by identifying and filtering out low-risk skin lesions.

2   Methods

2.1   Patient Data

We used the HAM10000 skin cancer dataset from Harvard Dataverse (https://dataverse.harvard.edu), which consisted of 10,015 multi-source, dermatoscopic images of common pigmented skin lesions [10]. This dataset also included descriptions of patient sex (54.0% male, 45.5% female, 0.5% unreported), age (mean of 51.9 years), the examination type (histopathology, follow-up appointment, expert consensus, *in vivo* confocal microscopy) and the location of the lesion on the body (back, lower extremity, trunk, etc.). Eighty percent of data was assigned to training and 20% of data was assigned to testing and validation subsets. Seven categories of skin lesions were separated into two classes (high-risk and low-risk), as shown in Table 1. These categories were used as model outputs for the classification task. Example images are shown in Fig. 1.

2.2   Data Augmentation and Balancing Classes

Data augmentation was used to balance the classification categories, which were originally distributed as shown in Fig. 2. To preserve the shape and margin of each image, rotation and flipping were applied.

Table 1. Skin lesion categories.

Class	Diagnostic category	Action
High-risk	Melanoma (mel), basal cell carcinoma (bcc), actinic keratoses (akiec), vascular lesions (vasc)	Inspection by patient and clinician
Low-risk	Melanocytic nevi (nv), dermatofibroma (df), benign keratosis-like lesions (bkl)	Filtered out of patient skin self-examination; diagnosis to be confirmed by clinician

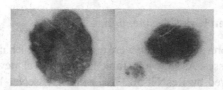

Fig. 1. Examples of melanocytic nevi (left) and melanoma (right) from the HAM10000 dataset.

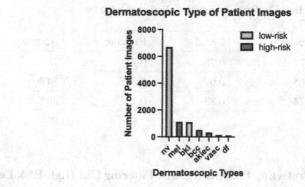

Fig. 2. Distribution of original data categories, including melanocytic nevi (nv), melanoma (mel), benign keratosis-like lesions (bkl), basal cell carcinoma (bcc), actinic keratoses (akiec), vascular lesions (vasc), and dermatofibroma (df).

2.3 Description of Models

Three convolutional neural network (CNN) architectures (ResNet-50, DenseNet-121, and VGG-16) were trained using the HAM10000 dataset to classify high-risk and low-risk skin lesions. ResNet-50 consisted of 48 convolutional layers, 1 maxpool, and 1 average pool layer. Imagenet weights and max pooling were used as parameters. A final softmax layer was added for the purpose of normalizing the CNN's output. DenseNet-121 was combined with batch normalization, dropout, a dense layer with a relu activation, and a dense layer with softmax activation. The VGG-16 is effective for applying transfer learning to computer vision image classification. To balance class distribution, the following class weights were added to the VGG-16: low-risk (1.0167) and potentially cancerous (0.794). Dropout was used as a form of regularization. Global average pooling was used to minimize overfitting through reducing model parameters. Early Stopping and Reduce Learning Rate on Plateau were selected as callbacks. Mini batches were used during training.

Each model was used to generate a prediction score ranging from 0 to 1, where 1 was classified as high-risk and 0 was classified as low-risk. Our classification objective was to help patients self-evaluate their lesions by accurately classifying low-risk images and minimizing the total number of lesions requiring patient examination.

3   Results

3.1   Accuracy of Lesion Risk Classification

Precision, recall, F1-score, and accuracy were evaluated for each model using argmax to distinguish between classes. As shown in Table 2, VGG-16 achieved the highest overall accuracy (80%), followed by ResNet-50 (78%) and DenseNet-121 (74%). From this initial accuracy assessment, VGG-16 was selected as the preferred model.

Table 2. Overall image prediction results.

Model	Precision	Recall	F1-score	Accuracy
ResNet-50	0.71	0.78	0.72	78%
DenseNet-121	0.65	0.69	0.66	74%
VGG-16	0.74	0.83	0.75	80%

3.2   Fine-Tuning for Protecting Patients Against Filtering Out High-Risk Lesions

Our next goal was to ensure that all high-risk lesions would remain within the pool of images assessed by a patient. To minimize the number of high-risk lesions incorrectly classified as low-risk, a threshold of 0.01 was selected for differentiating classes, shifting predictions that were greater than 0.01 into the high-risk bracket. In other words, lesions would only be placed in the low-risk category if they were high-confidence predictions. As shown in Table 3, shifting the threshold between classifications resulted in filtering 50.7% of images. We observed that 98.4% of these filtered images were known to be low-risk lesions. Furthermore, 96.2% of all potentially cancerous images were correctly classified as high-risk lesions, while the remaining 3.8% of high-risk images (8/213) were incorrectly classified as low-risk lesions.

Table 3. Evaluation of classification effectiveness (threshold of 0.01).

Model	Percentage of workload removed for patient	Precision of low-risk category	Recall of high-risk lesions	Fraction of high-risk lesions incorrectly classified
ResNet-50	27.1%	0.967	0.958	9/213
DenseNet-121	33.5%	0.976	0.962	8/213
VGG-16	50.7%	0.984	0.962	8/213

4 Discussion

This work demonstrated promising potential to reduce the number of lesions a patient must routinely monitor, while ensuring 98.4% of these filtered lesions are low-risk. By simplifying the process of skin self-examination, this approach minimizes the likelihood of a cancerous lesion being missed in the interval between clinical examinations. For patients who wish to be thorough, timely, and involved with their skin self-examinations, this work provides a tool for monitoring lesions at any frequency of the user's choosing and prompts clinical care when needed. This approach empowers patients to manage their own skin health in a timely and organized manner.

There are a few measures that would improve effective implementation of this approach in the future. Access to a larger variety of data across a spectrum of patient demographics would improve model training and utility in a clinical setting. Any algorithm should be tested on a wider demographic before being integrated into a clinical setting to consider factors such as potential skin-tone bias. With these adjustments, this tool can be applied to ease stress and improve efficiency during skin self-examinations, prompting patients to seek clinical help when needed.

5 Conclusion

To improve skin self-examination efficiency and reduce stress for patients, low-risk lesions were filtered from patient workflow. A skin cancer classifier was created that removed 50.70% of images with a precision value of 0.98 in the low-risk category and a recall value of 0.96 for high-risk lesions. This was achieved with a classification threshold of 0.01, using an image classification VGG-16 neural network that outperformed alternative ResNet-50 and DenseNet-121 models. Identifying low-risk lesions can potentially reduce the psychological stress associated with skin self-examinations, while encouraging patients to seek clinical help for high-risk lesions. This computation tool is complementary to clinician-based examinations, supporting patients in the intervals between their regular clinical visits.

Acknowledgements. This work was supported in part by the Department of Defense through the Breast Cancer Research Program under award number W81XWH-18-1-0342, the National Institutes of Health (NIH) National Library of Medicine T15 LM007033, the NIH National Cancer

8   K. Anderson and S. S. Hori

Institute R25 CA217729, and the Stanford Office of the Vice Provost for Undergraduate Education (VPUE). This work is licensed under a Creative Commons Attribution 4.0 International Public License (https://creativecommons.org/licenses/by/4.0/).

References

1. American Cancer Society. Cancer facts & figures (2021). https://www.cancer.org/cancer/skin-cancer.html. Accessed 1 Oct 2021
2. Guy, G.P., Jr., Thomas, C.C., Thompson, T., Watson, M., Massetti, G.M., Richardson, L.C., et al.: Vital signs: melanoma incidence and mortality trends and projections - United States, 1982–2030. MMWR Morb. Mortal. Wkly. Rep. **64**(21), 591–596 (2015)
3. Dorrell, D.N., Strowd, L.C.: Skin cancer detection technology. Dermatol. Clin. **37**(4), 527–536 (2019). https://doi.org/10.1016/j.det.2019.05.010
4. Linares, M.A., Zakaria, A., Nizran, P.: Skin cancer. Prim Care **42**(4), 645–659 (2015). https://doi.org/10.1016/j.pop.2015.07.006
5. Manne, S.L., et al.: Prevalence and correlates of skin self-examination practices among cutaneous malignant melanoma survivors. Prev. Med. Rep. **19**, 101110 (2020). https://doi.org/10.1016/j.pmedr.2020.101110
6. Yagerman, S., Marghoob, A.: Melanoma patient self-detection: a review of efficacy of the skin self-examination and patient-directed educational efforts. Expert. Rev. Anticancer Ther. **13**(12), 1423–1431 (2013). https://doi.org/10.1586/14737140.2013.856272
7. Adegun, A.A., Viriri, S.: FCN-based DenseNet framework for automated detection and classification of skin lesions in dermoscopy images. IEEE Access **8**, 150377–150396 (2020). https://doi.org/10.1109/ACCESS.2020.3016651
8. Mobiny, A., Singh, A., Van Nguyen, H.: Risk-aware machine learning classifier for skin lesion diagnosis. J. Clin. Med. **8**(8), (2019). https://doi.org/10.3390/jcm8081241
9. Jutzi, T.B., et al.: Artificial intelligence in skin cancer diagnostics: the patients' perspective. Front. Med. (Lausanne) **7**, 233 (2020). https://doi.org/10.3389/fmed.2020.00233
10. Tschandl, P., Rosendahl, C., Kittler, H.: The HAM10000 dataset, a large collection of multi-source dermatoscopic images of common pigmented skin lesions. Sci. Data **5**, 180161 (2018). https://doi.org/10.1038/sdata.2018.161

Predictive Signatures for Lung Adenocarcinoma Prognostic Trajectory by Multiomics Data Integration and Ensemble Learning

Hayan Lee[1](✉), Gilbert Feng[2], Ed Esplin[1], and Michael Snyder[1](✉)

[1] Department of Genetics, Stanford University, Stanford, CA, USA
{hayan.lee,explain,mpsnyder}@stanford.edu
[2] Electrical Engineering and Computer Sciences, University of California, Berkeley, Berkeley, CA, USA
gilbertfeng@berkeley.edu

Abstract. Lung cancer is the most prevalent cancer worldwide. About 80% to 85% of lung cancers are non-small cell lung cancer (NSCLC). One of the major types of NSCLC is lung adenocarcinoma (LUAD), which solely accounts for approximately 40% of all cases. Although there has been a dramatic therapeutic improvement, the prognostic trajectory has relied on primarily clinical features such as tumor-nodal-metastasis (TNM) stage, age upon diagnosis, and smoking history for decades. It does not reflect molecular alterations on its pathway or heterogeneity of tumorigenesis. Here we propose an integrative multi-omics random forest model to predict survival time for LUAD patients. We identified multi-omics signatures with higher importance to better predict survival time than clinical annotations that physicians traditionally use. We confirmed that the integrative prediction model outperforms any single-omic-based model. We discovered that a methylation-based model performed best among any single-omic-based model for LUAD since it provides the most abundant signature candidates. Although methylation assay is costly in general, paradoxically, methylation offers the most economical pool as prognosis markers due to more abundant assay points.

Keywords: Survival time prediction · Integrative multi-omics model · Machine learning

1 Introduction

Lung cancer is the most prevalent cancer in many countries worldwide and has two subtypes: small cell lung cancer and non-small cell lung cancer, the latter of which comprises about 80–85% of lung cancers [1, 2]. Lung adenocarcinoma (LUAD) is one of the major subtypes of non-small cell lung cancer, the only subtype in never smokers [3], along with lung squamous cell carcinoma (LUSC). LUAD accounts for approximately 40% of all lung cancer cases.

Prediction of its prognostic trajectory is important, especially to each patient. Traditionally prognostic trajectory has been estimated by clinical data, such as ages upon diagnosis, stage, and smoke history. This method is inaccurate because it does not consider

© Springer Nature Switzerland AG 2021
G. Bebis et al. (Eds.): ISMCO 2021, LNBI 13060, pp. 9–23, 2021.
https://doi.org/10.1007/978-3-030-91241-3_2

molecular characteristics in its pathway. Kaplan-Meier estimates provide the simplest and predictable way given the selected factor but cannot associate with related other factors and cannot be expressed as a functional form [4]. The Cox proportional hazards model can handle multiple variables and is realistic in that the hazard ratio changes over time, but it is not predictable to estimate survival time [5]. Recently there has been a dramatic improvement in treatment by molecule-targeting therapies. However, its prediction is not accurate enough because it still relies solely on clinical annotation and does not take molecular responses into account. Some data integration effort was made by incorporating gene expression data [6, 7]. Epigenetics data also have been exploited [8, 9]. There has been an effort to have even more omics data involved but most ended up with algorithmic integration rather than omics-level data integration [10].

Thus, we propose an ensemble learning method on high-dimensional omics data with clinical annotation to predict survival time. We learned a random forest regression (RFR) model [11, 12] exploiting the Cancer Genome Atlas (TCGA) LUAD multi-omics data and clinical annotations [13, 14]. To build a survival time prediction model, 'Days to death' was selected as the prediction target. Random forest regression, an ensemble of multiple decision trees, was selected to learn a model across heterogeneous data types since it does not require normalizing features, while other machine learning algorithms usually do. Random forest regression also can deal with nonlinear solution space and a nonparametric model, which does not require any assumptions about the data distribution. Thus, it is ideal for our integrative nonlinear prediction model learning.

Long term vs. short term survival classification has been studied more preferably since two group classification is comparatively easier than multi-group classification or regression [15–17]. Yu et al. performed classification of long-term vs. short-term survival of non-small cell lung cancer patients but exploited mainly hematoxylin and eosin (H&E) histological image data with a few omics markers of interest [18]. Li et al. identified eight genes relating to survival in LUAD using only gene expression data [19]. Yu et al. learned a prediction model to classify short-term ($<$3yr) and long-term ($>$3yr) survival from LUAD using only somatic mutational features [20]. An integrative prediction model suggested RNA-seq should be more predictable on prognostics of survival time than other genomic data types but still failed to include the methylation data that eventually causes gene expression change. We extended omics data integration from conventional clinical history to methylation, gene expression, and protein abundance from TCGA LUAD patients.

2 Inherent Characteristics of Multi-omics Data

TCGA has generated a variety of omics data along with clinical annotations. TCGA detailed molecular levels on various cancer types and collected methylation, gene expression, protein abundance along with genomic data such as copy number variation (CNV), somatic mutation, and microRNA expression. The previous studies show that gene expression was the most predictable omics data type among clinical, gene expression, CNV, somatic mutation, microRNA expression, and protein abundance, but it failed to include methylation data [20]. Thus we integrated methylation, gene expression, and protein data along with clinical annotation to see if methylation data is more predictable than gene expression data.

TCGA LUAD collected six types of omics data from ~500 patients. About 20% of them have survival time annotations. Methylation data is already normalized by its assay design. We performed log normalization for gene expression data, and proteome data were also Z-score normalized. To further reduce model learning time, we performed feature engineering using Pearson correlation coefficients (PCC) [21, 22]. The preprocess reduced the original data matrix to 1/1000–1/2 (Fig. 1).

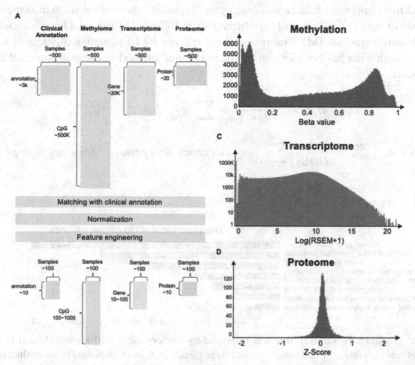

Fig. 1. Methylation, gene expression, and protein distribution from TCGA LUAD naturally vary. It presents that each omics data has its unique distribution signature. Accordingly, normalization should be adopted for prediction model learning. (A) For LUAD, TCGA collected data from ~500 patients and provided ~500K CpG methylation, ~20K gene expression, ~200 protein, and 100 clinical annotations, including 'Days to death', the target phenotype. (B) The distribution of the methylome (C) The distribution of transcriptome (D) The distribution of proteins.

3 Single-Omics Prediction Model

3.1 Conventional Clinical History Based Model as a Baseline

Clinical annotation data were retrieved from TCGA. We selected patients who had the 'Days to death' annotation and then selected other clinical history features that were recorded for all those patients such as 'number_pack_years_smoked'. Roughly ~50 clinical annotations were available for model learning. Since 50 features do not hurt the learning efficiency, we trained a model with all 50 clinical features without further feature selection.

Feature importance in random forest is formulated in (1) and (2); that is each feature x can change prediction accuracy compared to random permutation of the feature x, tested in out-of-bag (OOB) data points. Feature importance of clinical annotation was displayed in Fig. 2, and overall performance was represented in Fig. 7. As expected, the most important feature is the smoking intensity which is represented in packs/years. The second most important feature was 'age upon diagnosis', then tumor stage information; primary tumor (T) was the most significant factor, followed by regional lymph node (N) and distant metastasis (M). The revealed importance by RFR were realistic and well-aligned with what has been known by the traditional method to estimate survival time by doctors.

$$Importance_x = \frac{1}{|all\ Tree|} \sum_{allTree} \Delta\ Accuracy_{Tree,x}^{OOB} \tag{1}$$

$$\Delta\ Accuracy_{Tree,x}^{OOB} = \frac{1}{|OOB_T|} \sum_{i \in OOB_T} Accuracy\ with\ perm_x - Accuracy\ w/o\ perm_x \tag{2}$$

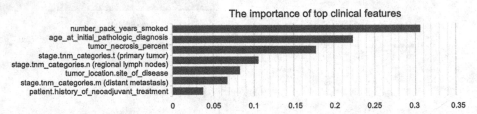

Fig. 2. Traditionally, survival time was estimated by doctors using well-known clinical history such as smoking intensity and time, age, and stage. Since PCC of clinical data is lower than other omics data, PCC thresholds were not applied. The RFR model learned from all clinical annotations and found that smoking intensity was the most important, followed by age, necrosis percentage, and tumor stage.

Clinical annotation-based RFR is selected as our baseline for the entire study. It is a strong baseline given that non-linear ensemble learning methods can address such complex heterogeneous data.

3.2 Methylome-Based Survival Time Prediction Model

For methylation, TCGA adopted Illumina Infinium HumanMethylation450K BeadChip (HM450) [23], where half a million CpGs were assayed to compute beta values, i.e., methylation ratio (which is the number of reads with methylated cytosine divided by the total number of reads). We extracted LUAD methylation data of the patients with 'Days to death'. the barcodes in the clinical annotation and the barcodes of the methylation file were compared to select only patients who have a 'Days to death' clinical annotation.

~100 patients were used for model training. The total number of assayed CpGs was ~485K. The beta value is already normalized as a ratio of 0 to 1. CpG loci that started with 'cg' were selected and the features with any missing data across the ~100 patients were excluded for model learning. The shape of the distribution of methylation data is bimodal (Fig. 1A), where CpGs are either highly methylated or unmethylated, which is very authentic compared to bell curve shares of transcriptome and proteome data.

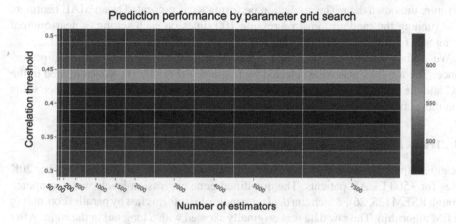

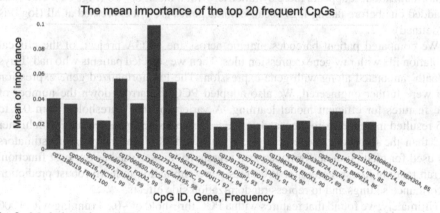

Fig. 3. Methylome-base RFR model prediction performance was grid-explored along with the number of estimators and PCC threshold (top). Since RFR includes a randomization process, we ran RFR >100 times. Thus the importance was averaged across 100 runs (bottom).

We employed mean absolute error (MAE) as our cost function [24]. We utilized 5-fold cross-validation to measure prediction model performance. To make model learning efficient and effective, we performed feature engineering by PCC. We computed PCC and set various thresholds from 0.3 to 0.5 to select features. PCC allowed us to reduce the number of features down to tens of thousands from half a million. Along with PCC, we also experimented with a varied number of estimators from 50 to 7500, and intervals set exponentially. We defined a parameter grid and ran random forest regression for each cell to search the parameter combination space for the best-performed model. Since the algorithm relies on randomization, we ran random forest regression 100 times per cell to obtain more robust performance results (Fig. 3). The best performance was shown with a PCC threshold of 0.4, and the number of estimators does not seem to affect the performance significantly. Note that selecting features with only high correlation does not always guarantee better prediction, as it may cause an overfitting issue where the learned model fitted too much with the current data set, thus becoming unreliable for the future unknown data. The prediction performance is presented as an MAE heatmap. After running the random forest regression 100 times on each setting, a near-optimal setting was found at a PCC threshold of 0.38 with 1500 estimators.

We further studied the CpGs that notably contributed to better prediction performance. The top 20 CpGs were selected by frequency (Fig. 3). The genes related to the CpG and the actual frequency are shown with a CpG ID. The average importance value is on the Y-axis.

3.3 Transcriptome-Based Ensemble-Learning Model

The gene expression data were also retrieved from TCGA. The data quantified over 20K genes for ~500 LUAD patients. The quantified gene expression levels were computed through RSEM [25, 26], which can deal with multiple isoforms fast by parallel computing the EM algorithm. The raw data was originally skewed with a long tail in the right. After log normalization, it appears more symmetric, with a mean of ~10 (Fig. 1C). Note that we added one before taking logs because some genes are not expressed at all (log 0 is not defined).

We compared patient barcodes, unique across the TCGA project, of the clinical annotation file with raw gene expression files. Then we selected patients who had 'Days to death' annotated along with gene expression. The log-normalized gene expression data were further engineered. We also adopted PCC to narrow down the number of gene features for efficient model learning. A variety of PCC thresholds from 0.2 to 0.45 resulted in hundreds to thousands of gene features since gene features with higher PCC than the thresholds were selected. Along with PCC, the number of estimators was used for prediction performance grid search. MAE was used as our cost function. We ran random forest regression 100 times per combination to learn robust prediction performance settings and to repress randomization side effects.

Ultimately, we found that features with a PCC threshold of ~0.34 running with 1000 estimators gave the lowest MAE. Overfitting degraded prediction performance when a few gene expression features with too high PCC were selected (Fig. 4). The average importance of the top 10 frequent genes is shown in Fig. 4 (bottom). KLHDC8B and DENND1A were shown in all 100 training and tests [27, 28].

3.4 Proteome-Based Model

Processed Reverse Phase Protein Array (RPPA) data were retrieved from TCGA [29]. The data described the quantified protein abundance of 364 patients for 225 proteins. The data was already normalized, as displayed in Fig. 1D. The normalized data file had to be further engineered. We compared patient barcodes, unique across the TCGA

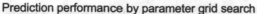

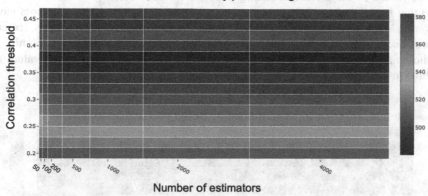

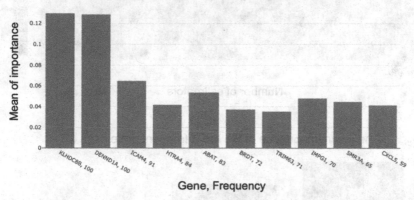

Fig. 4. The transcriptome-based RFR model prediction performance was grid-searched along with the number of estimators and PCC threshold (top). The top 10 genes by frequency are represented, and the mean importance was computed across 100 runs (bottom).

project, of the clinical annotation file with the normalized protein abundance file. Then we selected patients who had annotated along with protein abundance levels.

We also adopted PCC to narrow down the number of gene features for efficient model learning. PCC between 'Days to death' and normalized protein abundance levels was computed. A variety of PCC thresholds from 0.1 to 0.3 resulted in tens of protein abundance features since protein features with higher PCC than the thresholds were selected. Along with PCC, the number of estimators was used for prediction performance grid search. MAE was used as our cost function. We ran 5-fold cross-validation to measure prediction performance. We ran random forest regression 100 times per combination to learn robust prediction performance settings and to suppress randomization side effects. The top 3 proteins (BID, CCT5, EEF2K) by frequency were represented [30–32].

The results of the parameter tuning were demonstrated in Fig. 5. Ultimately, we found that features with a PCC threshold of ~0.28 running with 4000 estimators gave the lowest MAE. Overfitting degenerated prediction performance when too few protein features due to extremely high PCC threshold were selected. Furthermore, too high a threshold may lose some of the informative features. The average importance values of the three most frequent proteins are shown in Fig. 5 (bottom).

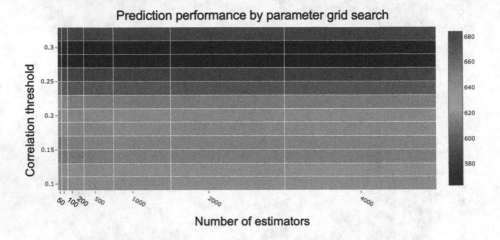

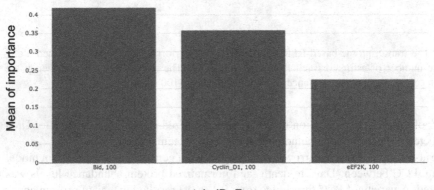

Fig. 5. Proteome-base RFR model prediction performance was grid-explored along with the number of estimators and PCC threshold (top). The top 3 proteins (BID, CCT5, EEF2K) by frequency were represented. The mean importance was computed across 100 runs (bottom).

4 Integrative Multi-omics Prediction Model

4.1 Integrative Modeling

We tried to find the intersection among methylation, gene expression, and protein abundance (Fig. 6). DKK1 and GFOD2 are confirmed by both methylation and gene expression data. Since there was a low amount of protein data available, none of the genes in methylation or gene expression data could be cross-confirmed by protein data.

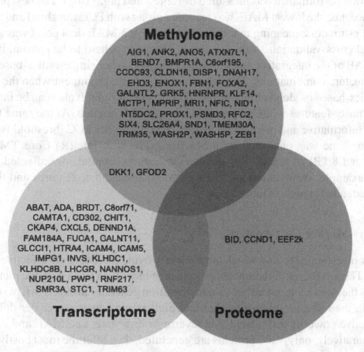

Fig. 6. We further investigated if there are any genes that two or more single omics-based models double confirmed. DKK1 and GFOD2 displayed significance in both methylation and gene expression data. Since TCGA generated only a handful of proteome data (~200), it was unlikely to confirm genes by proteomic data.

This inspired us to further develop an integrative model with all the heterogeneous omics data and the clinical annotations. We again chose random forest regression because it can handle non-linear solution space and does not require intense normalization. We selected features across the three omics data and the clinical annotations by PCC thresholds. We learned a model, measured prediction performance after 5-fold cross-validation, and plotted the prediction performance as MAE.

Firstly, the integrative model outperformed any single omics-based prediction model across all PCC thresholds (Fig. 7). For single-omics-based models, the methylation-based model performed best, followed by the gene expression-based model. These two single-omic-based models predict better than traditional survival time estimates based on smoke history, tumor stage, and age upon diagnosis. It is partly because having more features gives a higher chance to come across better predictor features. Note that the clinical annotation-based model was more robust than the protein-based model, even though protein provides more features than clinical annotations in general.

Prediction performance was measured in Table 1 and Fig. 7 (top). The best prediction performance, i.e., the lowest MAE, was recorded along with PCC threshold and a various number of estimators, meaning that decision trees. Each MAE data point was averaged after 5-fold cross-validation. Although the significance is hard to be proven, it is clear that the MAE of the integrative model is lower than any other single-omics-based model across all feature combinations. The improvement is more prominent when the MAE of single-omics-based models is higher in the far left and far right. It also can be interpreted that more noisy features when a lower PCC threshold is applied. At the same time, we lose more informative and predictable features when a higher PCC threshold is applied.

Running time was measured on a MacBook Pro with Intel(R) Core TM core i5 processor and 8 GB of RAM. The number of features significantly affected learning time. For example, methylation had the most marker candidate features and thus took the most extended runtime (Table 2).

4.2 Omics-Marker Cost Analysis

We further investigated to find which omics data provide the most cost-effective markers (Table 3). Though the methylation and protein cost more than RNA-seq, the methylation platform is the most economical because methylation generates millions of CpG markers, resulting in the lowest total cost/marker and highest predictive power per dollar [33]. The predictive power is formulated as a reverse or error rate, i.e., MAE and computed (3). Comparatively, only ~200 proteins are generated, thus offer the most costly marker.

$$Predictive\ power = \frac{1}{MAE} \tag{3}$$

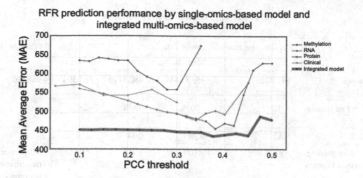

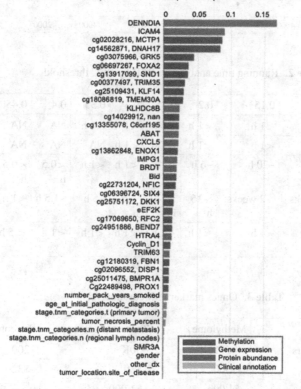

Fig. 7. RFR prediction performance from 5-fold cross-validation shows that the clinical data-based prediction model, our baseline, performs better than the protein-based model. However, it also reveals that the gene expression or methylation-based model can outperform traditional survival time estimates. The integrated multi-omics data prediction model outperforms any other models that rely solely on one type of omics data or clinical data (top). The mean importance values of the top 40 features by frequency are shown after 100 runs and 5-fold cross-validation. Interestingly, the top two features are from gene expression, followed by methylation features. We identified ~20 omics features more significantly predictable than traditional clinical features (bottom).

Table 1. Prediction performance

	Clinical annotation	Omics data			Integrative model
		Methylation	RNA	Protein	
Best performance (the lowest MAE)	547.0829	456.8844	480.5176	563.304	436.8226
# of features before feature engineering	~3K	~500K	~30K	~2K	~100
PCC threshold	NA	0.38	0.34	0.28	0.375
# features used for training models (at optimal Pearson threshold)	~50	<100	<100	<10	Methylome: ~20 Transcriptome ~10 Proteome <10 Clinical annotation ~10
# features with high importance	<10	~30	~10	<10	~10
# estimators	4000	7500	1000	4000	2000

Table 2. Running time analysis of RFR by PCC threshold

	0.1	0.15	0.2	0.25	0.3	0.35	0.4	0.45	0.5
Protein	<1 h	<1 h	<1 h	<1 h	<1 h	<1 h	NA	NA	NA
Clinical	<1 h	<1 h	<1 h	<1 h	<1 h	NA	NA	NA	NA
RNA	>48 h	~20 h	~6 h	~2 h	<1 h	<1 h	<0.5 h	<0.5 h	NA
Methylation	>2 weeks	>2 weeks	>36 h	>24 h	~15 h	~5 h	~1.5 h	<1 h	<1 h
Integrative model	<1 h	<1 h	<1 h	<1 h	<1 h	<1 h	<1 h	<.5 h	<0.5 h

Table 3. Omics marker unit cost analysis

	Methylome	Transcriptome	Proteome
Total number of markers	~4.5M	~30K	~200
Library cost [34]	>$300	~$80	~$320
Sequencing cost	~$1,000	~$1,000	0
Total cost/marker	~$0.0029	~$0.036	~$1.60
Best MAE	456.8844	480.5176	563.304
Predictive power/USD($)	2.87	2.25	0.57

5 Discussion and Future Works

In this study, we used a random forest regression, non-parametric ensemble learning method, to predict the survival time of lung adenocarcinoma (LUAD) patients from heterogeneous omics data and clinical annotations. We specifically chose LUAD because it is widely accepted that smoking history is one of the most important factors to estimate survival time, along with other clinical factors such as age and tumor stage. Our goal was to identify omics markers that outperform such clinical markers, which have previously been the most reasonable factors in predicting survival time, and we successfully found such better-predicting omics markers, such as DENND1A, ICAM4, cg02038216 (MCTP1), cg03075966 (GRK5), cg06697267 (FOXA2), etc. [35] It is observed that DENND1A is overexpressed in LUAD patients [36]. ICAM4 was identified as methylation markers by Wang et al. [37].

In the future, it would be interesting to apply RFR to other types of cancer data from TCGA to see (1) if methylation markers consistently outperform gene expression markers and (2) if there are any common methylation/gene expression markers to predict survival time and (3) if the prediction power can be improved by adding image data, which is available to LUAD patients.

Acknowledgments and Funding. The authors thank Akshay Sanghi for discussing the significance of smoking history in lung cancer patients. This work used the Genome Sequencing Service Center by Stanford Center for Genomics and Personalized Medicine Sequencing Center, supported by the grant award NIH S10OD020141.

References

1. Lung Carcinoma: Tumors of the Lungs. Merck Manual Professional Edition, Online Edition. Accessed 12 Aug 2021
2. What Is Lung Cancer? Types of Lung Cancer. https://www.cancer.org/cancer/lung-cancer/about/what-is.html. Accessed 12 Aug 2021
3. Subramanian, J., Govindan, R.: Lung cancer in never smokers: a review. J. Clin. Oncol. **25**(5), 561–570 (2007)
4. Goel, M.K., Khanna, P., Kishore, J.: Understanding survival analysis: Kaplan-Meier estimate. Int. J. Ayurveda Res. **1**, 274–278 (2010)
5. Katzman, J.L., et al.: DeepSurv: personalized treatment recommender system using a Cox proportional hazards deep neural network. BMC Med. Res. Methodol. **18** (2018). Article number: 24
6. West, M., et al.: Predicting the clinical status of human breast cancer by using gene expression profiles. Proc. Natl. Acad. Sci. **98**, 11462–11467 (2001)
7. Van't Veer, L.J., et al.: Gene expression profiling predicts clinical outcome of breast cancer. Nature **415**, 530–536 (2002)
8. Yu, X., et al.: Predicting lung adenocarcinoma disease progression using methylation-correlated blocks and ensemble machine learning classifiers. PeerJ **9**, e10884 (2021)
9. Cao, W., et al.: Multi-faceted epigenetic dysregulation of gene expression promotes esophageal squamous cell carcinoma. Nat. Commun. **11** (2020). Article number: 3675

10. Kwek, S., Nguyen, C.: iBoost: boosting using an instance-based exponential weighting scheme. In: Elomaa, T., Mannila, H., Toivonen, H. (eds.) Machine Learning: ECML 2002, pp. 245–257. Springer, Heidelberg (2002). https://doi.org/10.1007/3-540-36755-1_21
11. Ho, T.K.: Random decision forests. In: Proceedings of 3rd International Conference on Document Analysis and Recognition (1995)
12. Ho, T.K.: The random subspace method for constructing decision forests. IEEE Trans. Pattern Anal. Mach. Intell. **20**, 832–844 (1998)
13. Cancer Genome Atlas Research Network, et al.: The cancer genome atlas pan-cancer analysis project. Nat. Genet. **45**, 1113–1120 (2013)
14. The Cancer Genome Atlas Research Network: Comprehensive molecular profiling of lung adenocarcinoma. Nature **511**, 543–550 (2014)
15. Campbell, K.R., Yau, C.: A descriptive marker gene approach to single-cell pseudotime inference. Bioinformatics **35**, 28–35 (2019)
16. Liu, L., et al.: Favorable outcome of patients with lung adenocarcinoma harboring POLE mutations and expressing high PD-L1. Mol. Cancer **17** (2018). Article number: 81
17. Nie, D., et al.: Multi-channel 3D deep feature learning for survival time prediction of brain tumor patients using multi-modal neuroimages. Sci. Rep. (2019). **9** Article number: 1103
18. Yu, K.-H., et al.: Predicting non-small cell lung cancer prognosis by fully automated microscopic pathology image features. Nat. Commun. **7** (2016). Article number: 12474
19. Li, S., et al.: Identification of an eight-gene prognostic signature for lung adenocarcinoma. Cancer Manag. Res. **10**, 3383–3392 (2018)
20. Yu, J., et al.: LUADpp: an effective prediction model on prognosis of lung adenocarcinomas based on somatic mutational features. BMC Cancer **19** (2019). Article number: 263. https://doi.org/10.1186/s12885-019-5433-7
21. National Cancer Institute: Pearson Correlation Coefficient. Definitions (2020)
22. Gooch, J.W.: Pearson correlation coefficient. In: Gooch, J.W. (ed.) Encyclopedic Dictionary of Polymers, pp. 990–990. Springer, New York (2011). https://doi.org/10.1007/978-1-4419-6247-8_15317
23. Infinium HumanMethylation450K BeadChip Product Files. https://support.illumina.com/array/array_kits/infinium_humanmethylation450_beadchip_kit/downloads.html
24. Chai, T., Draxler, R.R.: Root mean square error (RMSE) or mean absolute error (MAE)? – Arguments against avoiding RMSE in the literature. Geosci. Model Dev. **7**, 1247–1250 (2014)
25. RSEM: accurate transcript quantification from RNA-Seq data with or without a reference genome. Bioinformatics 69–102 (2014). https://doi.org/10.1201/b16589-9
26. Teng, M., et al.: A benchmark for RNA-seq quantification pipelines. Genome Biol. **17**, 203 (2016)
27. Expression of KLHDC8B in lung cancer - The Human Protein Atlas. http://www.proteinatlas.org/ENSG00000185909-KLHDC8B/pathology/lung+cancer/LUAD. Accessed 12 Aug 2021
28. Zengin, T., Önal-Süzek, T.: Analysis of genomic and transcriptomic variations as prognostic signature for lung adenocarcinoma. BMC Bioinformatics **21**, 368 (2020)
29. Reverse phase protein microarray (reverse phase protein array, RPPA, 'reverse phase array'). The Dictionary of Genomics, Transcriptomics and Proteomics 1 (2015)
30. Billen, L.P., Shamas-Din, A., Andrews, D.W.: Bid: a Bax-like BH3 protein. Oncogene **27**, S93–S104 (2008)
31. Meng, Y., et al.: CCT5 interacts with cyclin D1 promoting lung adenocarcinoma cell migration and invasion. Biochem. Biophys. Res. Commun. **567**, 222–229 (2021)
32. Expression of EEF2K in lung cancer. The Human Protein Atlas. https://www.proteinatlas.org/ENSG00000103319-EEF2K/pathology/lung+cancer/LUAD. Accessed 12 Aug 2021
33. Epigenomics Core @ WCMC. http://epicore.med.cornell.edu/pricelist.ph. Accessed 12 Aug 2021

34. Infinium MethylationEPIC Kit. https://www.illumina.com/products/by-type/microarray-kits/infinium-methylation-epic.html
35. Li, C., Long, Q., Zhang, D., Li, J., Zhang, X.: Identification of a four-gene panel predicting overall survival for lung adenocarcinoma. BMC Cancer **20**, 1198 (2020)
36. McAllister, J.M., et al.: Overexpression of a DENND1A isoform produces a polycystic ovary syndrome theca phenotype. Proc. Natl. Acad. Sci. U. S. A. **111**, E1519–E1527 (2014)
37. Wang, R., Zhu, H., Yang, M., Zhu, C.: DNA methylation profiling analysis identifies a DNA methylation signature for predicting prognosis and recurrence of lung adenocarcinoma. Oncol. Lett. **18**, 5831–5842 (2019)

The Role of Hydrophobicity in Peptide-MHC Binding

Arnav Solanki[1] (ID), Marc Riedel[1]([✉]) (ID), James Cornette[2], Julia Udell[1,3] (ID),
Ishaan Koratkar[4], and George Vasmatzis[3] (ID)

[1] University of Minnesota, Minneapolis, MN 55455, USA
{solan053,mriedel,udell008}@umn.edu
[2] Iowa State University, Ames, IA 50011, USA
cornette@iastate.edu
[3] Center for Individualized Medicine, Biomarker Discovery Group, Mayo Clinic,
Rochester, MN 55902, USA
Vasmatzis.George@mayo.edu
[4] Eagan High School, Eagan, MN 55123, USA
ishaan@koratkar.com

Abstract. Major Histocompability Complex (MHC) Class I molecules
provide a pathway for cells to present endogenous peptides to the immune
system, allowing it to distinguish healthy cells from those infected by
pathogens. Software tools based on neural networks such as NetMHC
and NetMHCpan predict whether peptides will bind to variants of MHC
molecules. These tools are trained with experimental data, consisting of
the amino acid sequence of peptides and their observed binding strength.
Such tools generally do not explicitly consider hydrophobicity, a significant biochemical factor relevant to peptide binding. It was observed
that these tools predict that some highly hydrophobic peptides will be
strong binders, which biochemical factors suggest is incorrect. This paper
investigates the correlation of the hydrophobicity of 9-mer peptides with
their predicted binding strength to the MHC variant HLA-A*0201 for
these software tools. Two studies were performed, one using the data
that the neural networks were trained on and the other using a sample
of the human proteome. A significant bias within NetMHC-4.0 towards
predicting highly hydrophobic peptides as strong binders was observed
in both studies. This suggests that hydrophobicity should be included in
the training data of the neural networks. Retraining the neural networks
with such biochemical annotations of hydrophobicity could increase the
accuracy of their predictions, increasing their impact in applications such
as vaccine design and neoantigen identification.

Keywords: MHC Class I · Peptide · Machine learning · Neural
networks

Supported by NSF Grant 2036064.

G. Bebis et al. (Eds.): ISMCO 2021, LNBI 13060, pp. 24–37, 2021.
https://doi.org/10.1007/978-3-030-91241-3_3

1   Introduction

The Human Leukocyte Antigen (HLA) gene system encodes cell-surface proteins that play a key role in the immune system. HLA proteins of Major Histocompatibility Complex (MHC) Class I allow nucleated cells to present peptides from within the cell. In these cells, endogenous proteins are eventually broken down into small peptides, 8–15 amino acids long, by the proteasome. These antigens are then trafficked to and loaded onto MHC Class I molecules. If sufficient binding affinity is achieved then a stable peptide-MHC (pMHC) complex is formed and transported to the cell surface. Self-peptides, antigens encoded in the human proteome, and foreign peptides, derived from pathogenic proteins, can thus be presented. By surveilling these extracellular pMHCs, CD8$^+$ T-cells can distinguish normal cells from pathogen-infected cells, and kill the latter.

The mechanics of peptide binding are specific to a given MHC variant. The HLA genes are among the most diverse in the human population [9]. Thus the set of all antigens presented by a person's MHCs, labelled as their *immunopeptidome*, is unique and determines the capacity of their immune system. Since the immune response of a person to, for instance, a viral infection like COVID-19 is dependent on whether the foreign antigens presented by their MHCs are distinguishable from self-peptides, understanding and predicting pMHC binding is an important topic. In this paper, we have focused on NetMHC-4.0 [2] and NetMHCpan-4.1 [25], two state-of-the-art neural network based methods that predict pMHC binding. Both software tools have been applied in predicting cancer immune escape mechanisms [17], checkpoint blockade immunotherapy for tumors [16], and identifying COVID-19 T-cell response targets [10].

While these tools provide valuable pMHC predictions, they do not model pMHC binding at the molecular level or capture the entire antigen presentation pathway's effects. Hydrophobicity is a measure of how repulsive a molecule is to water, often a consequence of nonpolarity. It plays a vital role in protein binding – for example, the MHC molecule HLA-A*0201 (A2) contains hydrophobic binding pockets that bind to correspondingly hydrophobic amino acids. Historically, immunopeptidomes have been predicted by modelling the interaction of the MHC binding pocket and peptide, particularly focusing on biochemical attributes such as sidechain conformations, solvation energies, electrostatic interactions, and hydrophobicity [30,32]. However with improved computing power, larger datasets, and the need for interpolation due to the high polymorphism in MHC Class I alleles [21], artificial intelligence based methods have become popular over such mechanistic means of prediction. As NetMHC-4.0 and NetMHCpan-4.1 are trained with sequence data and binding scores only, they lack the means of modelling these biochemical attributes. Other software tools such as ANN-Hydro [6] have utilized hydrophobicity in their immunogenic predictions, but do not predict binding affinity and are outperformed by NetMHCpan [18]. In our use of NetMHC-4.0 we observed a prevalence of highly hydrophobic peptides in the predicted A2 immunopeptidome. We found this unintuitive, since peptides in which all amino acids are hydrophobes would not dissolve in the aqueous cytosol within the cell and would thus likely not be available for binding with the MHC. We therefore sought to investigate the possibility that these tools were over-estimating binding scores for such hydrophobic peptides. We conducted two analyses on both NetMHC-4.0 and NetMHCpan-4.1, one using training data and the other using a sample of the human proteome, to investigate the correlation of predicted strong binders and hydrophobicity. We present our results and highlight the unintended bias within NetMHC-4.0 for predicting highly hydrophobic peptides as strong binders.

2   Methods

NetMHC and NetMHCpan allow users to input a list of peptides or whole proteins, and test the binding of all peptides within a chosen MHC molecule. Both tools return an adjusted score between 0 (for non binders) and 1 (for strong binders) for all peptides. A notable distinction between the two is that NetMHC is limited to predicting binding for MHC variants it is trained on, i.e. curated MHCs. In contrast, NetMHCpan is capable of interpolating predictions for uncurated MHCs if users provide the MHC amino acid sequence. This is achieved through the integration of MHC sequence as a data feature in training, and by a larger training dataset generated using a sophisticated machine learning method called NNAlign_MA [1]. NetMHCpan-4.1 consists of an ensemble of 50 neural networks, each with hidden layers containing 55 and 66 neurons, that were trained using 5-fold cross validation. NetMHC-4.0 consists of 20 neural networks, each with a single hidden layer of 5 neurons, that were trained using a nested 5-fold cross validation approach [2].

2.1   Data Mining

NetMHC-4.0 was trained on $CD8^+$ epitope binding affinity (BA) data from the Immune Epitope Database. This data provides binding scores for peptides to single allele MHCs, with a score that is scaled between 0 and 1 that measures how strongly the peptide binds. NetMHCpan-4.1 was trained on BA data and additional eluted ligand (EL) data from mass spectrometry experiments from multiple sources [25]. The EL data includes multi-allele information that was deconvoluted into single allele datapoints using NNAlign_MA. EL score is binary (either 0 or 1) since it checks if a peptide is present in a MHC's immunopeptidome. The training data for NetMHCPan-4.1 is provided here.

This cumulative dataset contained more than 13 million pMHC data points, that we filtered down to the 52569 9-mers interacting with HLA-A02:01 (A2) and labelled as set TRN. 9-mers were the most frequent length of antigens in human immunopeptidomes, and A2 was the most frequent MHC in the training dataset. The distribution of all binding scores in TRN is shown in Fig. 1. Please note that Fig. 1 contains two distinct graphs, the second being independently sorted to visualize the cumulative distribution, as discussed in the caption. All peptides from TRN were fed into NetMHC-4.0 to obtain their predicted BA scores, and

then filtered for strong binders predicted by the tool's default 0.5% rank threshold. This set of predicted strong binding peptides by NetMHC-4.0 was labelled
as NSB (NetMHC Strong Binders). Similarly, the strong binders predicted by
NetMHCpan-4.1 from TRN based on their EL scores were compiled into the set
PSB (NetMHCPan Strong Binders).

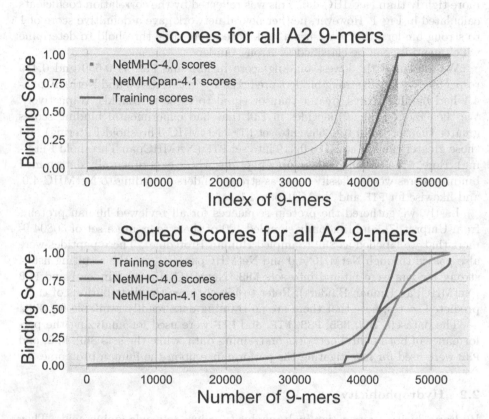

Fig. 1. Binding scores for all A2 9-mers in the NetMHCpan-4.1 training set TRN in blue,
NetMHC-4.0 Binding Affinity predicted scores in red, and NetMHCpan-4.1 Eluted
Ligand predicted scores in yellow. The top graph has been sorted on the training data,
and for each peptide index the NetMHC, NetMHCpan, and training scores are plotted
at that x coordinate. The Pearson correlation coefficient between the training scores
and NetMHC-4.0 was 0.8492, and between the training scores and NetMHCpan-4.1 was
0.863. In the bottom graph, each plot of scores was independently sorted to demonstrate
their cumulative distributions. Note that here the order of peptides is not conserved
across the 3 plots in the bottom graph. (Color figure online)

From the scores shown in the second graph of Fig. 1, it was clear that the
pMHC binding data for A2 9-mers fitted a mostly binary data classification
problem, since only 15% peptides had a training score not equal to 0 or to 1.
This was mostly due to the addition of EL data which provided a binary "yes" or

"no" answer to whether a given peptide was found attached to A2 through mass spectroscopy. NetMHC-4.0 predicted scores, shown in red, were mostly located in between the extremes of 0 and 1 due to the smaller training data consisting of only BA assay data. It seemed that NetMHCpan-4.1, shown in yellow, was much better at estimating non-binders (scores of 0), and fitted the S-curve transition more tightly than NetMHC-4.0. This was reflected by the correlation coefficients calculated in Fig. 1. However, neither neural network gave a definitive score of 1 to strong binders; they both use a rank based percentile threshold to determine which peptides can be classified as strong binders.

We measured the lowest binding score in NSB and PSB as 0.659 and 0.419 respectively – i.e. all strong binders predicted by NetMHC-4.0 and NetMHCpan-4.1 had binding scores greater than or equal to these thresholds, respectively. We then filtered for all peptides in TRN that had experimental binding scores greater than or equal to 0.659 into set NTF (NetMHC Threshold Filtering) and those greater than or equal to 0.419 into set PTF (NetMHCpan Threshold Filtering). Here, NTF contained all training peptides whose experimentally determined binding scores would classify them as strong binders according to NetMHC-4.0, and likewise for PTF and NetMHCpan-4.1.

Lastly, we gathered the protein sequences for all reviewed human proteins from Uniprot [7], and randomly sampled 100 of them to create a set of 50804 9-mers that we labelled as SHP (Sampled Human Proteome). These peptides were also passed through NetMHC-4.0 and NetMHCpan-4.1, and the resulting list of strong binders were filtered into sets NHB (NetMHC Human Binders) and PHB (NetMHCPan Human Binders). Refer to Fig. 2 to see the distributions of these predicted scores; note that there are no training data readily available for SHP.

The datasets TRN, NSB, PSB, NTF, and PTF were used for analyzing the performance of both neural networks on training data, while the sets SHP, NHB, and PHB were used for investigating the performance upon the human proteome.

2.2　Hydrophobicity

Hydrophobicity scales assign hydrophobicity values to single amino acids. They are designed so the hydrophobicity of long peptides or protein chains can be estimated by simply linearly adding up the scores of their constituent amino acids. While scales such as Kyte-Doolittle [14], Cornette [8], and Hopp-Woods [11] are commonly used, we settled on the Moon scale [20] for calculating hydrophobicity in our analyses. This newer scale differs from the scales listed above in that it specifically focuses on the sidechain hydrophobicity and polarity of single amino acids. Unlike the other scales, which are well suited for protein folding problems that do not correlate with sidechain hydrophobicity [19], the Moon scale is more representative of how small peptides would behave in an aqueous solution. The scale ranks the 20 amino acids in decreasing order of hydrophobicity as follows: F (1.43), L (1.26), I (1.15), P (1.13), Y (0.94), V (0.80), M (0.79), W (0.63), A (0.46), C (0.24), E (−0.27), G (−0.30), T (−0.33), S (−0.35), D (−0.85), Q (−0.88), N (−1.08), R (−1.19), H (−1.65), K (−1.93). For any given 9-mer, we calculated its total hydrophobicity by adding up the values for each of its 9 amino acids as

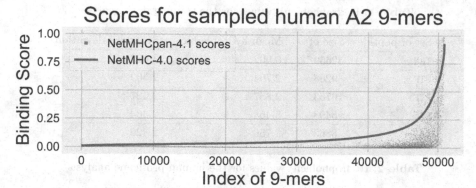

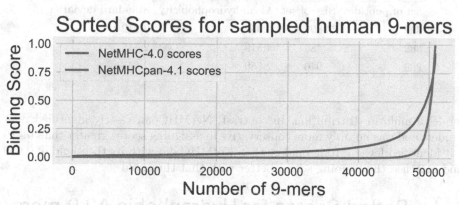

Fig. 2. Predicted binding scores for all 9-mers in the 100 sampled human proteins in SHP, according to NetMHC-4.0 in blue, and NetMHCpan-4.1 in red. In the top graph, the sequence of peptides is conserved for both sequences and sorted by NetMHC scores. In the bottom graph, both sequences are independently sorted and the sequence of peptides is not conserved across both sequences. (Color figure online)

reported by the scale. For a given set of peptides, we measured the mean and standard deviation of the hydrophobicity scores of all peptides in it. Refer to Tables 1 and 2 for these measurements.

2.3 Hydrophobicity Filtering

An additional filter we applied was for peptides that were entirely hydrophobic. For this, we only accepted peptides from TRN and SHP that had all 9 amino acids with a Moon hydrophobicity score greater than 0.46 (i.e. that of Alanine). This meant that the resulting sets of peptides were made entirely of Phenylalanine, Leucine, Isoleucine, Proline, Tyrosine, Valine, Methionine, and Tryptophan – highly hydrophobic and nonpolar amino acids. For TRN, only 55 such peptides were found. The training scores and predicted scores for these are shown in Fig. 3. While the training data in blue showed non-binders, strong binders, and some in between, NetMHC predicted no decisive non-binders and instead seemed to

Table 1. Hydrophobicity values for the training data analysis

Set of peptides	Size of set	Mean hydrophobicity	Standard deviation
TRN	52659	0.902	3.063
NTF	9268	2.794	2.502
PTF	10763	2.857	2.527
NSB	6498	3.458	2.364
PSB	8863	2.756	2.426

Table 2. Hydrophobicity values for the human proteome analysis

Set of peptides	Size of set	Mean hydrophobicity	Standard deviation
SHP	50804	0.052	3.212
NHB	486	4.519	2.515
PHB	940	2.789	2.645

model a uniform distribution. In contrast, NetMHCpan clearly identified non-binders and was notably more conservative in assigning scores greater than 0.419 – it identified fewer strong binders than NetMHC did with its threshold of 0.659 and matched the training scores better with that threshold.

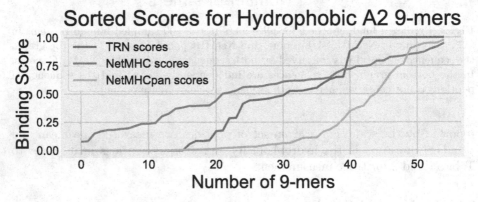

Fig. 3. Binding scores for all highly hydrophobic 9-mers in TRN in blue, and the predicted scores by NetMHC-4.0 in red and NetMHCpan-4.1 in yellow. All of the 3 plots were independently sorted to demonstrate their distributions. Peptides were considered hydrophobic if all their amino acids were more hydrophobic than Alanine. (Color figure online)

For SHP, 33 hydrophopbic 9-mers were found. Their predicted binding scores by both neural networks are shown in Fig. 4. Once again, the NetMHC scores in blue appeared almost linear and seemed to be uniformly distributed, while

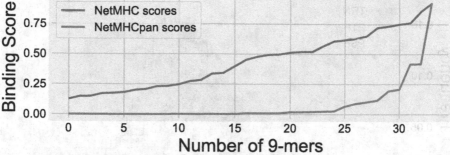

Fig. 4. Predicted Binding scores for all highly hydrophobic 9-mers in SHP, with NetMHC-4.0 in blue, and NetMHCpan-4.1 in red. Both plots were independently sorted to demonstrate their distributions. Peptides were considered hydrophobic if all their amino acids were more hydrophobic than Alanine. (Color figure online)

NetMHCpan in red clearly identified lots of non-binders, and fewer strong binders (about 3).

2.4 2 Sample t-Test

For any 2 given sets of sampled numbers, the 2 Sample t-Test allows for comparing their means. Given an arbitrary set S_i with mean μ_i, standard deviation σ_i, and sample size n_i, the t-statistic for two sets S_i and S_j can be computed as

$$t_{i,j} = \frac{(\mu_i - \mu_j)}{\sqrt{(\sigma_i^2/n_i) + (\sigma_j^2/n_j)}}.$$

For all our named sets, we conducted a cross-set 2 sample t-Test using Python's scipy.stats package to determine how likely shifts in the means of hydrophobicity scores for sets could be due to random sampling. This computer package also calculated p-values, enumerating the probability of the two compared sets having unequal means purely by chance, from the t-statistic.

3   Results

Consider the histograms of the hydrophobicity scores of all peptides in the datasets TRN, PTF, and PSB shown in Fig. 5. The 52,659 peptides in TRN model a gaussian distribution centered at mean hydrophobicity of 0.9. The other two sets containing high binders according to NetMHCpan, PTF and PSB, shift to the right with new means at 2.8 and 2.7 respectively. The shift towards more hydrophobic 9-mers is not unexpected – as the authors of NetMHC [2,22] depict in the A2 logos here, locations 2 and 9 in the A2 immunopeptidome 9-mers strongly favor

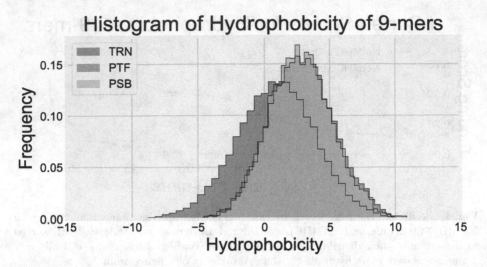

Fig. 5. Histogram of the Hydrophobicity scores (on the x-axis) for sets TRN (in blue), PTF (in red), and PSB (in yellow). Note how PTF and PSB are similar distributions. Refer to Sect. 2.2 for details. (Color figure online)

amino acids such as Leucine, Methionine, Valine, and Isoleucine. The reservation of these 2 locations with these hydrophobic amino acids corresponds roughly to 2.0 shift in Moon hydrophobicity. The two sets possess comparable means and standard deviations, visually and quantitatively as shown in Table 1.

In contrast, let us now focus on how NetMHC performed in a similar analysis. In Fig. 6, the histograms for TRN, NTF, and NSB are shown. The set NTF in red, consisting of peptides with experimentally measured binding scores greater than 0.659, is centered at a mean of 2.8. However set NSB in yellow, containing peptides that NetMHC predicted as strong binders, is offset to the right with a mean of 3.4. This shift in the distribution of NSB points out an increase in hydrophobicity of 9-mers that bind to A2. That is, NetMHC predicts the A2 immunopeptidome to be more hydrophobic than the experimental data, or even NetMHCpan's predictions, suggest.

Looking at the histograms of the SHP, NHB, and PHB – i.e. the human proteome sampled 9-mers and the strong binders predicted by the neural networks from them – this shift in hydrophobicity increases. In Fig. 7, the SHP distribution is centered at about 0 (SHP and TRN do not share the same mean, which we suspect is due to the Moon hydrophobicity scale being normalized on human proteins). As in Fig. 5, the strong binders predicted by NetMHCpan are slightly hydrophobic, resulting in a shift in the mean to 2.8 (similar to PTF and PSB). However, the strong binders predicted by NetMHC in the human proteome are much more hydrophobic, with a shifted mean at 4.5. The gain in hydrophobicity from SHP to NHB implied by this shift is even larger than the shift observed in

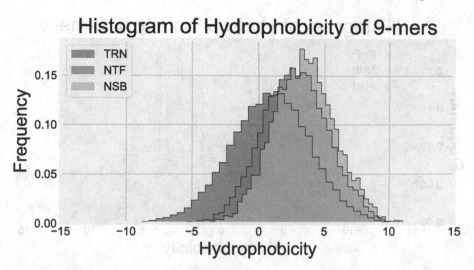

Fig. 6. Histogram of the Hydrophobicity scores (on the x-axis) for sets TRN (in blue), NTF (in red), and NSB (in yellow). Clearly, NTF and NSB do not align, with NSB shifted towards being more hydrophobic. (Color figure online)

Fig. 6. Once again NetMHC overestimates how hydrophobic the A2 immunopeptidome is, and performs worse in the human proteome evaluation compared to the training data.

The cross set T-test tested the equivalence of two given sets with p-values. The smaller the p-value, the more likely the two sets have unequal means. We clustered the sets based on the p-values from the cross set t-test. The clustering criteria were: 1) two sets chosen from separate clusters should have a p-value lower than 0.001; and 2) a set should have a p-value greater than 0.001 with at least one set in its cluster. We obtained the following 5 clusters of sets: (TRN), (SHP), (NTF, PTF, PSB, PHB), (NSB), and (NHB). The first two clusters cover the sets that were put in to the neural networks, TRN and SHP. The third cluster includes NetMHCpan's predicted immunopeptidomes and the experimentally observed immunopeptidome. The largest observed p-value in this cluster was 0.961 between NTF and PHB. The fourth and fifth clusters cover the set of predicted strong binders according to NetMHC for the training data analysis and the human proteome analysis respectively. The clusters signify how similar sets within them are, and how different they are to sets outside that cluster. As the NSB and NHB sets occupying their own clusters, the t-test highlights that NetMHC's predictions do not match up with the experimental immunopeptidomes and with NetMHCpan's predictions. These different analyses confirm the increased hydrophobicity of strong binding 9-mers from NetMHC's prediction, and expose an unintended bias in the neural network's performance compared to NetMHCpan.

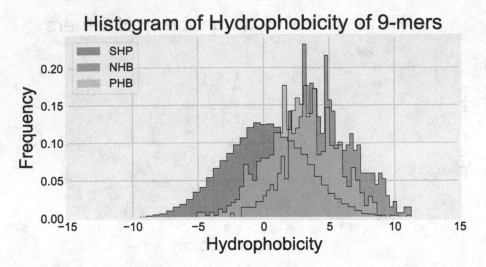

Fig. 7. Histogram of the Hydrophobicity scores (on the x-axis) for sets SHP (in blue), NHB (in red), and PHB (in yellow). Clearly, NHB and PHB do not align, with NHB shifted towards being more hydrophobic. (Color figure online)

4   Conclusion

Imagine a toy example of a hydrophilic box filled with water, containing a single HLA-A*0201 protein and a completely hydrophobic 9-mer of LMIPFFILL. The peptide would be repelled by the aqueous medium and latch itself to the A2 protein. Now consider the cell interior, where the highly hydrophobic 9-mer would be repelled by the cytosol and stick to whatever mildly hydrophobic surface it finds nearby. This 9-mer would no longer be trafficked to any MHC for binding, and would not be presented as an antigen on the cell surface despite the 2nd and 9th amino acids highly favoring A2 binding. This cherry-picked peptide was a non-binding peptide (EL score of 0) in the NetMHCpan-4.1 training dataset but was predicted as a strong binder by NetMHC-4.0 for A2 (BA score of 0.792). In general, we do not expect completely hydrophobic antigens to populate any MHC's immunopeptidome. This example illustrates how the MHC antigen presentation pathway do not support NetMHC's prediction. Coupled with our observations in Sect. 3 we conclude that NetMHC has a statistically significant bias towards predicting hydrophobic peptides as strong binders to A2. NetMHC may provide accurate binding affinity predictions, but does not correctly reflect the composition of the A2 immunopeptidome with regards to hydrophobicity. This bias suggests a false positive prediction problem, and limits the utility of NetMHC in applications such as vaccine design [28] and neoantigen identification [15].

In contrast, NetMHCpan-4.1 does not show a similar bias, potentially due to its larger training data set and the use of MHC amino acid sequence as a data feature of the neural network. The MHC sequence could be allowing the neural network to infer and model the binding mechanics of the A2 binding pockets.

Furthermore, eluted ligand data might allow NetMHCpan to capture aspects of the entire antigen presentation pathway instead of estimating pMHC binding strength alone. Lastly, the generated negative data in the training data [1] could be lowering the predicted scores for hydrophobic non-binders.

Changes could be implemented in future iterations of NetMHC to address this bias, such as:

- Augmenting training data to include information on hydrophobicity of constituent amino acids. This would entail adding an extra dimension or feature to the training data that stores hydrophobicity scores. We recommend the Moon Hydrophobicity scale for this purpose.
- Incorporating better negative data in training, and properly populating the training dataset with more peptides from the human proteome. Note the offset mean hydrophobicity of TRN compared to SHP in Tables 1 and 2, suggesting that the current training data does not accurately represent the human proteome.
- Designing a post-processing filter that can separate out false positives based on hydrophobicity calculations.

Our emphasis is not on reverse engineering a neural network or trying to divine molecular information from predicted values. Instead, we are highlighting the importance of biochemical attributes pertinent to pMHC binding and cellular machinery. A more insightful neural network, like NetMHCpan-4.1, will avoid false positives and will potentially allow for better performance and greater impact in applications. In future work, we will focus on identifying more significant structural and mechanistic attributes that pose hurdles for AI-based methods. We are developing a structural prediction tool capable of predicting peptide binding with uncurated MHC molecules.

References

1. Alvarez, B., et al.: NNAlign_MA; MHC peptidome deconvolution for accurate MHC binding motif characterization and improved T-cell epitope predictions. Mol. Cell. Proteomics **18**(12), 2459–2477 (2019)
2. Andreatta, M., Nielsen, M.: Gapped sequence alignment using artificial neural networks: application to the MHC class I system. Bioinformatics **32**(4), 511–517 (2016)
3. Bassani-Sternberg, M., Pletscher-Frankild, S., Jensen, L.J., Mann, M.: Mass spectrometry of human leukocyte antigen Class I peptidomes reveals strong effects of protein abundance and turnover on antigen presentation. Mol. Cell. Proteomics **14**(3), 658–673 (2015)
4. Bonsack, M., et al.: Performance evaluation of MHC Class-I binding prediction tools based on an experimentally validated MHC-peptide binding data set. Cancer Immunol. Res. **7**(5), 719–736 (2019)
5. Calis, J.J., et al.: Properties of MHC class I presented peptides that enhance immunogenicity. PLoS Comput. Biol. **9**(10), e1003266 (2013)
6. Chowell, D., et al.: TCR contact residue hydrophobicity is a hallmark of immunogenic CD8+ T cell epitopes. Proc. Natl. Acad. Sci. **112**(14), E1754–E1762 (2015)

7. Consortium, U.: UniProt: a worldwide hub of protein knowledge. Nucl. Acids Res. **47**(D1), D506–D515 (2019)
8. Cornette, J.L., et al.: Hydrophobicity scales and computational techniques for detecting amphipathic structures in proteins. J. Mol. Biol. **195**(3), 659–685 (1987)
9. Gourraud, P.A., et al.: HLA diversity in the 1000 genomes dataset. PLoS ONE **9**(7), e97282 (2014)
10. Grifoni, A., et al.: Targets of T cell responses to SARS-CoV-2 coronavirus in humans with COVID-19 disease and unexposed individuals. Cell **181**(7), 1489–1501 (2020)
11. Hopp, T.P., Woods, K.R.: A computer program for predicting protein antigenic determinants. Mol. Immunol. **20**(4), 483–489 (1983)
12. Huang, L., Kuhls, M.C., Eisenlohr, L.C.: Hydrophobicity as a driver of MHC Class I antigen processing. EMBO J. **30**(8), 1634–1644 (2011)
13. Jurtz, V., Paul, S., Andreatta, M., Marcatili, P., Peters, B., Nielsen, M.: NetMHCpan-4.0: improved peptide-MHC class I interaction predictions integrating eluted ligand and peptide binding affinity data. J. Immunol. **199**(9), 3360–3368 (2017)
14. Kyte, J., Doolittle, R.F.: A simple method for displaying the hydropathic character of a protein. J. Mol. Biol. **157**(1), 105–132 (1982)
15. Lancaster, E.M., Jablons, D., Kratz, J.R.: Applications of next-generation sequencing in neoantigen prediction and cancer vaccine development. Gene. Test. Mol. Biomark. **24**(2), 59–66 (2020)
16. Łuksza, M., et al.: A neoantigen fitness model predicts tumour response to checkpoint blockade immunotherapy. Nature **551**(7681), 517–520 (2017)
17. McGranahan, N., et al.: Allele-specific HLA loss and immune escape in lung cancer evolution. Cell **171**(6), 1259–1271 (2017)
18. Mei, S., et al.: A comprehensive review and performance evaluation of bioinformatics tools for HLA class I peptide-binding prediction. Brief. Bioinform. **21**(4), 1119–1135 (2020)
19. Monera, O.D., Sereda, T.J., Zhou, N.E., Kay, C.M., Hodges, R.S.: Relationship of sidechain hydrophobicity and α-helical propensity on the stability of the single-stranded amphipathic α-helix. J. Peptide Sci. **1**(5), 319–329 (1995)
20. Moon, C.P., Fleming, K.G.: Side-chain hydrophobicity scale derived from transmembrane protein folding into lipid bilayers. Proc. Natl. Acad. Sci. **108**(25), 10174–10177 (2011)
21. Nielsen, M., Andreatta, M., Peters, B., Buus, S.: Immunoinformatics: predicting peptide-MHC binding. Ann. Rev. Biomed. Data Sci. **3**, 191–215 (2020)
22. Nielsen, M., et al.: Reliable prediction of T-cell epitopes using neural networks with novel sequence representations. Protein Sci. **12**(5), 1007–1017 (2003)
23. Paul, S., Grifoni, A., Peters, B., Sette, A.: Major histocompatibility complex binding, eluted ligands, and immunogenicity: benchmark testing and predictions. Front. Immunol. **10**, 3151 (2020)
24. Peters, C., Elofsson, A.: Why is the biological hydrophobicity scale more accurate than earlier experimental hydrophobicity scales? Proteins: structure. Function Bioinform. **82**(9), 2190–2198 (2014)
25. Reynisson, B., Alvarez, B., Paul, S., Peters, B., Nielsen, M.: NetMHCpan-4.1 and NetMHCIIpan-4.0: improved predictions of MHC antigen presentation by concurrent motif deconvolution and integration of MS MHC eluted ligand data. Nucl. Acids Res. **48**(W1), W449–W454 (2020)

26. Sarkizova, S., et al.: A large peptidome dataset improves HLA class I epitope prediction across most of the human population. Nat. Biotechnol. **38**(2), 199–209 (2020)
27. Schmidt, J., Guillaume, P., Dojcinovic, D., Karbach, J., Coukos, G., Luescher, I.: In silico and cell-based analyses reveal strong divergence between prediction and observation of T-cell-recognized tumor antigen T-cell epitopes. J. Biol. Chem. **292**(28), 11840–11849 (2017)
28. Schubert, B., Brachvogel, H.P., Jürges, C., Kohlbacher, O.: EpiToolKit-a web-based workbench for vaccine design. Bioinformatics **31**(13), 2211–2213 (2015)
29. Simm, S., Einloft, J., Mirus, O., Schleiff, E.: 50 years of amino acid hydrophobicity scales: revisiting the capacity for peptide classification. Biol. Res. **49**(1), 1–19 (2016)
30. Vasmatzis, G., Zhang, C., Cornette, J.L., DeLisi, C.: Computational determination of side chain specificity for pockets in class I MHC molecules. Mol. Immunol. **33**(16), 1231–1239 (1996)
31. Wieczorek, M., et al.: Major histocompatibility complex (MTC) class I and MHC class II proteins: conformational plasticity in antigen presentation. Front. Immunol. **8**, 292 (2017)
32. Zhang, C., Vasmatzis, G., Cornette, J.L., DeLisi, C.: Determination of atomic desolvation energies from the structures of crystallized proteins. J. Mol. Biol. **267**(3), 707–726 (1997)
33. Zhang, Y.H., Xing, Z., Liu, C., Wang, S., Huang, T., Cai, Y.D., Kong, X.: Identification of the core regulators of the HLA I-peptide binding process. Sci. Rep. **7**(1), 1–11 (2017)

Spatio-Temporal Tumor Modeling and Simulation

Simulating Cytotoxic T-Lymphocyte and Cancer Cells Interactions: An LSTM-Based Approach to Surrogate an Agent-Based Model

David Bernard[1] , Anthony Kobanda[1] , and Sylvain Cussat-Blanc[1,2](✉)

[1] University of Toulouse, IRIT CNRS UMR5505, Toulouse, France
sylvain.cussat-blanc@ut-capitole.fr
[2] Artificial and Natural Intelligence Toulouse Institute (ANITI), Toulouse, France

Abstract. Through an Agent-based model (ABM) it is possible to compute simple and basic behaviours at the cellular scale, while observing the emergence of complex conducts or patterns at the population scale. Thus, in this modeling paradigm, macroscopic phenomena can be explained by a set of behaviors of the agents. However, due to the high computational cost, the exploration of the parameters of these models for the optimization or calibration of protocols is still an open challenge. In this paper, we propose a surrogate model based on an Long-Short Term Memory (LSTM) neural network to replicate the predictions of an ABM much faster. The ABM used in this paper models the interactions between cytotoxic T-lymphocytes (CTL) and cancer cells [8]. The initial results shows that the neural network is capable of reproducing the emergent behavior of the ABM with a reduced computational cost.

Keywords: Surrogate modelling · LSTM · T-lymphocyte · Cancer

1 Introduction

The study of CTL is crucial in the development of therapeutic cancer strategies [4]. Unfortunately research on this matter requires many time-lapse microscopy acquisitions to gather enough key information. To expand on the understanding of CTL, we have proposed in a previous work [8] an ABM of their interactions with cancer cells. In this model, target cancer cells (melanoma cells) are attacked by CTL which are scooting in the environment in order to kill all target cells. To develop this initial model interactively with biologists, we used a state-transition diagram and high-quality visualisation to assess the qualitative quality of the model (see Fig. 1). Furthermore, our model is calibrated and validated with *in vitro* biological data: it reproduces overnight kinetics of the CTL fight against target cells at different CTL/Target cells ratios.

This work is funded by the BMS foundation and the Canceropole Grand Sud-Ouest.

G. Bebis et al. (Eds.): ISMCO 2021, LNBI 13060, pp. 41–46, 2021.
https://doi.org/10.1007/978-3-030-91241-3_4

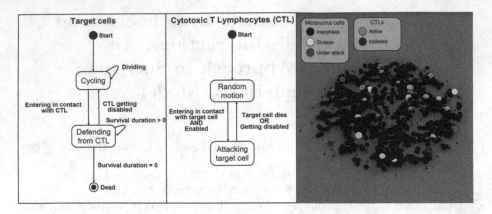

Fig. 1. Distribution of the amount of CTL from the dataset generation. A. Total amount of CTL injected. B. Amount of CTL for an injection.

In the study aforementioned, it was shown that a same amount of CTL injected over time shows greater lytic ability than a single injection at the beginning of a cell culture (usual protocol). To study the impact of more complex injection kinetics, a large number of simulations is required. However, despite a relatively short computation time compared to biological experiments (1 min per simulation of 18 h with 1000 initial cancer cells), the exploration of such a search space remains computationally costly.

Hence, in order to replicate the model's behaviour while reducing its computational cost, we propose in this paper to use a surrogate models, more commonly used in physics and engineering [5,13]. Due to the sequential nature of the injections, we propose to use an LSTM-based approach to reproduce the ABM outputs in shorter computational times.

2   Method

The ABM presented in [8] allowed to generate 200,000 simulations to train and test our model on. Each simulation has 18 inputs, representing the amount of CTL injected each hour, and 18×2 outputs corresponding to the number of dead and alive D10 cancer cells (isolated from metastatic melanoma patients [7]).

2.1   Dataset Generation

The simulations were constrained to not exceed a 1:1 effector/target (E/T) ratio. Figure 2 shows that using such a ratio, uniformly distributed in time, kills all cancer cells. It is therefore not necessary to explore kinetics with a higher ratio.

To avoid biases in the model while exploring as widely as possible the 18 dimensions injection kinetics' space, we used a Latin Hypercube Sampling (LHS) method [11]. It allows to generate a near-random sample of parameters value and to better cover the multidimensional domain considered. To take into account the

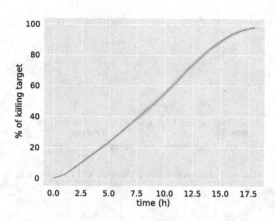
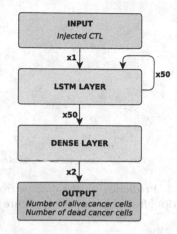

Fig. 2. Result of 10 simulations using ABM showing the percentage of tumor cells killed by CTL with an injection of 55 CTL each hour.

Fig. 3. Architecture of the surrogate model.

1:1 E/T limit ratio constraint while using the LHS, an additional dimension was introduced, containing the total amount of CTL injected over the span of a simulation. To obtain a convenient sequence, the first 18 values are normalized and multiplied by the value contained in the last dimension. Such a method allows to produce a dataset with a uniform distribution of the total CTL quantities and a distribution of the number of CTL per hour. Running the 200,000 simulations required 2 days and 19 h with an Intel® Xeon® E5-2660 v3 CPU (40 cores).

2.2 LSTM-Based Surrogate Model Architecture

LSTM networks are a particular type of recurrent neural networks [6], capable of learning dependencies in time-series data structures to perform forecasting [10]. Hence, due to the sequential and temporal nature of the data considered, LSTM networks are appropriate in order to develop the desired surrogate model.

The model considers the amount of CTL added at a time step and predicts the amount of dead and alive cancer cells at the next time step. The architecture of the model (Fig. 3) is made of an LSTM layer (input size 1, output size 50) and a dense layer (input 50 size, output 2 size). An Adam optimizer and a Mean Square Error (MSE) as the loss were used. The dataset was split with 80% of training data and 20% test data. 100 epochs were necessary to reach an MSE of 0.00029 both on the training and the testing dataset. The training required 5 min using a NVIDIA® Quadro® P620 GPU.

3 Results

3.1 The Model Can Reproduce the Predictions of the ABM

The surrogate model is able to predict the amount cancer cells over time. To observe the quality of the predictions made, three simulations with different

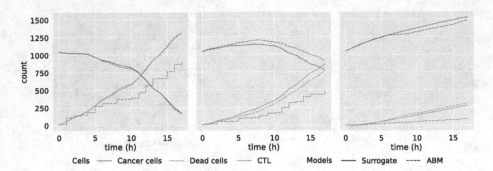

Fig. 4. Prediction on simulations from the test dataset with different CTL injection kinetics (dashed green) (Color figure online).

injection kinetics were selected (Fig. 4). We can observe that the trend of the predictions corresponds to the one proposed by the ABM and thus that the surrogate model is a good approximation of the ABM.

The predictions made are based on the new number of CTL injected as well as on model's memory of previous steps. Figure 5 shows the relative error at each time step. If the prediction made by the LSTM is diverging over time, the relative error remains reasonable as it only represent 2.25% of the global cancer cell population (dead and alive) in average of deviation from the ABM.

3.2   The Model Can Predict Kinetics Unseen During the Training

To validate the consistency of the model, it was confronted 10 times to a longer injection kinetic (40 h) with an 100 CTL injected every 4 h. Figure 6 shows that it indeed remains stable. The higher deviation beyond 30 h is due to the fact that the data do not contain simulations reaching such a number of dead cells.

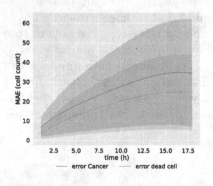
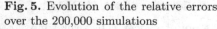

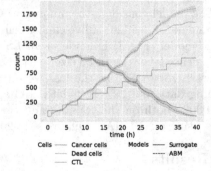

Fig. 5. Evolution of the relative errors over the 200,000 simulations

Fig. 6. Prediction of the model on a kinetic not represented in the dataset

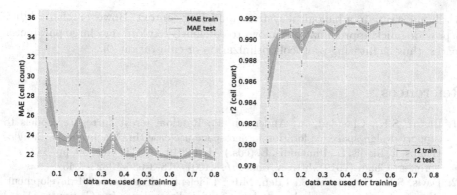

Fig. 7. Scores (A: Mean Absolute Errors, B: R2) obtained by the models with different ratios of the dataset included in the training split. For each rate, the dataset was shuffled and randomly separated into training and testing sets. Models are trained for 100 epochs. This was repeated 30 times for each training/testing ratios.

3.3   A Reduced Dataset Size Can Be Sufficient

To study of the performance according to the amount of data used, we proceeded 10 times as it follows. For each split ratio, a model is initialized and trained over a fraction of the dataset according to the ratio considered. The Fig. 7 shows that the data required was overestimated. Note that the model does not overfit, regardless of the size of the training dataset.

4   Discussion and Conclusion

We developed an LSTM-based surrogate model able to reproduce the kynetics of the ABM in various cases, seen and unseen during the training. A major benefit of such an approach is its very low computational cost in comparaison to ABM: whereas the generation of the dataset (200,000 simulations) required 2 days and 19 h, the LSTM-based neural network only required 5 min of training and less than two seconds to calculate the prediction of these 200k simulations.

Despite the attention paid to the dataset generation method, it is not free of bias. It would be relevant to explore other strategies such as Sobol's method, which seems to offer better results than LHS [2] to generate the dataset. Furthermore, although LSTM is a standard for time series modelling, other types of models from machine learning strategies can be considered, such as support vector regression (SVR) [3], random forest (RF) [1] or more conventional methods for building surrogate models like Kriging [12] and Gaussian Processes [14]. An open question is also how such a LSTM-based surrogate model can capture the stochasticity of the ABM model.

The proposed model could be extended to take into account additional parameters such as certain cellular characteristics and thus propose a generic surrogate not depending on a cell line. The use of surrogate models interfaced with an ABM is still quite rare in a biological systems modeling context. However, their ability to provide quick approximations allows to efficiently explore very large parameter spaces, thus facilitating protocol optimization or calibration [9].

References

1. Dasari, S.K., Cheddad, A., Andersson, P.: Random forest surrogate models to support design space exploration in aerospace use-case. In: MacIntyre, J., Maglogiannis, I., Iliadis, L., Pimenidis, E. (eds.) AIAI 2019. IAICT, vol. 559, pp. 532–544. Springer, Cham (2019). https://doi.org/10.1007/978-3-030-19823-7_45
2. Davis, S.E., Cremaschi, S., Eden, M.R.: Efficient surrogate model development: impact of sample size and underlying model dimensions. In: Computer Aided Chemical Engineering, vol. 44, pp. 979–984. Elsevier (2018)
3. Fan, Y., Lu, W., Miao, T., An, Y., Li, J., Luo, J.: Optimal design of groundwater pollution monitoring network based on the SVR surrogate model under uncertainty. Environ. Sci. Pollut. Res. **27**(19), 24090–24102 (2020). https://doi.org/10.1007/s11356-020-08758-5
4. Farhood, B., Najafi, M., Mortezaee, K.: CD8$^+$ cytotoxic T lymphocytes in cancer immunotherapy: a review. J. Cell. Physiol. **234**(6), 8509–8521 (2019)
5. Gu, H., Xu, Y.P., Ma, D., Xie, J., Liu, L., Bai, Z.: A surrogate model for the Variable Infiltration Capacity model using deep learning artificial neural network. J. Hydrol. **588**, 125019 (2020)
6. Hochreiter, S., Schmidhuber, J.: Long short-term memory. Neural Comput. **9**(8), 1735–1780 (1997)
7. Khazen, R., Müller, S., Gaudenzio, N., Espinosa, E., Puissegur, M.P., Valitutti, S.: Melanoma cell lysosome secretory burst neutralizes the CTL-mediated cytotoxicity at the lytic synapse. Nat. Commun. **7**(1), 1–15 (2016)
8. Khazen, R., Müller, S., Lafouresse, F., Valitutti, S., Cussat-Blanc, S.: Sequential adjustment of cytotoxic T lymphocyte densities improves efficacy in controlling tumor growth. Sci. Rep. **9**(1), 1–11 (2019)
9. Lamperti, F., Roventini, A., Sani, A.: Agent-based model calibration using machine learning surrogates. J. Econ. Dyn. Control **90**, 366–389 (2018)
10. Tian, Y., Pan, L.: Predicting short-term traffic flow by long short-term memory recurrent neural network. In: 2015 IEEE International Conference on Smart City/SocialCom/SustainCom (SmartCity), pp. 153–158. IEEE (2015)
11. Viana, F.A.: A tutorial on Latin hypercube design of experiments. Qual. Reliab. Eng. Int. **32**(5), 1975–1985 (2016)
12. Wang, H., Zhu, X., Du, Z.: Aerodynamic optimization for low pressure turbine exhaust hood using kriging surrogate model. Int. Commun. Heat Mass Transf. **37**(8), 998–1003 (2010)
13. van de Weg, B.P., Greve, L., Andres, M., Eller, T., Rosic, B.: Neural network-based surrogate model for a bifurcating structural fracture response. Eng. Fract. Mech. **241**, 107424 (2021)
14. Zhou, J., Turng, L.S.: Process optimization of injection molding using an adaptive surrogate model with Gaussian process approach. Polym. Eng. Sci. **47**(5), 684–694 (2007)

General Cancer Computational Biology

Strategies to Reduce Long-Term Drug Resistance by Considering Effects of Differential Selective Treatments

Tina Ghodsi Asnaashari and Young Hwan Chang[✉]

Department of Biomedical Engineering and Computational Biology Program,
Oregon Health and Science University, Portland, USA
chanyo@ohsu.edu

Abstract. Despite great advances in modeling and cancer therapy using optimal control theory, tumor heterogeneity and drug resistance are major obstacles in cancer treatments. Since recent biological studies demonstrated the evidence of tumor heterogeneity and assessed potential biological and clinical implications, tumor heterogeneity should be taken into account in the optimal control problem to improve treatment strategies. Here, first we study the effects of two different treatment strategies (i.e., symmetric and asymmetric) in a minimal two-population model to examine the long-term effects of these treatment methods on the system. Second, by considering tumor adaptation to treatment as a factor of the cost function, the optimal treatment strategy is derived. Numerical examples show that optimal treatment decreases tumor burden for the long-term by decreasing rate of tumor adaptation over time.

Keywords: Tumor heterogeneity · Optimal control · Cancer treatment

1 Introduction

Optimal control theory has been applied to reduce tumor burden when treatment is applied to the system [1–3]. In general, these methods proposed mathematical models and focused on identifying the optimal treatment regime or strategy that can drive the tumor population to a desired level so as to penalize excessive usage of the drug or minimize drug resistance [4]. For instance, in [1], the authors considered cancer therapy with application of one drug and determined the optimal regime that minimized the tumor burden while maintaining the normal cell population above a prescribed level. In other studies, the optimal drug adjustment is proposed to minimize the number of cancerous cells by considering different controlled combinations of administering the chemotherapy agents [2] or a mathematical model of tumor-immune interactions with chemotherapy is proposed [3].

Despite recent advances in modeling and cancer therapy using optimal control theory, tumor heterogeneity continues to be a major barrier for the successful treatment of cancer [5]. Many biological studies reported experimental evidence

© Springer Nature Switzerland AG 2021
G. Bebis et al. (Eds.): ISMCO 2021, LNBI 13060, pp. 49–60, 2021.
https://doi.org/10.1007/978-3-030-91241-3_5

for the existence of heterogeneity, discussed their impact on management of cancer and assessed potential biological and clinical implications [5–7]. Some studies proposed mathematical models to consider different cell population dynamics [8–11]. For instance, in [8], the authors proposed a state transition model of tumor cells and demonstrated different cell transition behavior across treatments to indicate how a tumor responds to treatments and is responsible for resistance.

To bridge the gap between the optimal control problem for minimizing tumor burden and understanding of tumor adaptation, tumor heterogeneity has been taken into account as an optimal control problem; an ordinary differential equation (ODE) model, which consists of sensitive and resistant cells to a certain drug, is proposed to determine drug administration schedules in order to avoid resistant population be dominant [12]. Although the authors considered reducing both resistant and sensitive sub-populations in their cost function, they did not explicitly consider drug-imposed selective pressures with respect to tumor heterogeneity. In [13], cell traits are considered to model how a resistant cell responds to a certain drug and are taken into account as levels of resistance in the cost function. The authors also reported that maximum tolerable dosage is not a good treatment strategy as it may lead to increase resistant cell population. In recent study [9], the authors modeled long-term effects of two different drug treatment methods; symmetric treatment method in which sub-population kill is equal and asymmetric treatment method that sub-population kill is unequal. Then, they performed simulation studies to analyze the effects of each parameter on therapeutic efficacy. Although they performed systematic simulation study with the sensitivity analysis by sweeping parameters to interrogate the effects of different drug-imposed selective pressures on long-term therapeutic outcome, it is limited to draw a fundamental understanding of the effect of differential selective pressure. Selective pressure is the influence exerted by drugs to promote one group of sub-population over another that may shift tumor heterogeneity distribution and generate resistance cells to the drug.

In this paper, motivated by [9], we first focus on a fundamental and principled understanding of the effect of differential selective treatments since they result in different tumor reduction rates over time and thus affect therapeutic outcome. Second, we formulate an optimal control problem to penalize a rate of tumor adaptation while minimizing tumor burden. Numerical simulations are introduced to demonstrate how tumor heterogeneity affects long-term effects with and without considering effects of differential selective treatments.

2   Background: Differential Selective Pressure Affects Long-Term Therapeutic Outcome

In the previous study [9], a simple two-population model has been studied to find out long-term effects of two different treatment regimes and demonstrated simulation result by showing the long-term effect of differential-imposed selective treatments. Such models are useful to show the general behaviour of biological systems. Herein, we summarize their work since we extend this study by focusing more theoretical analyses.

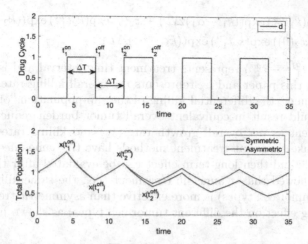

Fig. 1. A comparison of total tumor population between symmetric and asymmetric treatment schemes. The top figure shows drug treatment cycle and the bottom figure shows the overall tumor population dynamics of both symmetric and asymmetric treatment respectively.

A minimal two-population was modeled as (x_1, x_2) with distinctive growth rates (k_1, k_2) and drug killing rates (α_1, α_2) respectively [9]. The kinetics of the two sub-populations were modeled using a simple ODE for exponential growth as follows:

$$\dot{x}_1 = k_1 x_1 - d\alpha_1 x_1$$
$$\dot{x}_2 = k_2 x_2 - d\alpha_2 x_2 \tag{1}$$

where drug treatment (d) is a Heaviside step function as shown in Fig. 1. In the problem setting [9], in order to examine long-term effects of two different treatment regimes, the authors assumed the same initial overall tumor growth and tumor reduction for the first treatment cycle (i.e., from t_1^{on} and t_1^{off} where t_1^{on} and t_1^{off} represent the start time point and the end time point of the first treatment respectively) of both symmetric and asymmetric treatment conditions. Thus, the boundary and constraint prior to treatment are followed by:

$$x_1(0) \exp(k_1 t_1^{on}) + x_2(0) \exp(k_2 t_1^{on}) = (x_1(0) + x_2(0)) \exp(k_s t_1^{on}) \tag{2}$$

where $x_1(0)$ and $x_2(0)$ represent the initial sub-population sizes respectively and k_s represents a single overall growth rate. Thus, during the initial untreated growth phase of the tumor, the total tumor size is equivalent to a single overall growth rate.

Similarly, the boundary and constraint following first round of drug treatment satisfy the following condition which confirms that cell population is the same after the first treatment cycle:

$$x_1(0) \exp(k_1 t_1^{on}) \exp((k_1 - \alpha_1)\Delta T) + x_2(0) \exp(k_2 t_1^{on}) \exp((k_2 - \alpha_2)\Delta T)$$
$$= (x_1(0) + x_2(0)) \exp(k_s t_1^{on}) \exp((k_s - \alpha_s)\Delta T) \tag{3}$$

where $\Delta T \triangleq (t_1^{off} - t_1^{on})$ represents treatment time interval and is assumed to be constant in this paper and α_s represents the overall killing rate. Thus, after the first treatment, the differential killing of the sub-populations of asymmetric treatment should result in equivalent overall tumor burden reduction of symmetric treatment as per overall growth rate (k_s) and killing rate (α_s). These constraints make sure that treatment methods have the same effects after first treatment cycle and then long-term effect can be evaluated after that. A simulation result showed that symmetric treatment (i.e., the same killing effect on the different tumor cell types) is more effective than asymmetric treatment (i.e., different killing effect on the different tumor cell types) as shown in Fig. 1.

3 Differential-Imposed Selective Treatments Result in Different Tumor Reduction Rates

In this section, motivated by the simulation study [9], we provide a theoretical analysis to interrogate the effects of different drug-imposed selective pressures and further consider how to integrate this information into treatment design. First, we consider a tumor reduction after each round in symmetric treatment.

Definition 1. *A tumor reduction (TR) rate after each round can be defined as follows:*

$$TR_k \triangleq \frac{x(t_k^{on}) - x(t_k^{off})}{x(t_k^{on})} \tag{4}$$

where TR_k represents a tumor reduction rate of the kth drug cycle, $x(t_k^{on})$ and $x(t_k^{off})$ represent total tumor population at time step t_k^{on} and t_k^{off} respectively as shown in Fig. 1.

Lemma 1. *For symmetric treatment (i.e., equal selective treatment), a tumor reduction after each round will be constant over time.*

Proof.

$$x(t_k^{off}) = x_1(t_k^{off}) + x_2(t_k^{off})$$
$$= x_1(t_k^{on}) \exp((k_1 - \alpha_1)\Delta T) + x_2(t_k^{on}) \exp((k_2 - \alpha_2)\Delta T)$$
$$= (x_1(t_k^{on}) + x_2(t_k^{on})) \exp((k_s - \alpha_s)\Delta T)$$

where $\Delta T \triangleq t_k^{off} - t_k^{on}$ is assumed to be constant over k and for symmetric treatment we assume that $k_1 - \alpha_1 = k_2 - \alpha_2 = k_s - \alpha_s$ (i.e., tumor reduction is equal). Therefore, for symmetric treatment, a tumor reduction rate is constant as follows:

$$TR_k^{sym} = 1 - \frac{x(t_k^{off})}{x(t_k^{on})} = 1 - \exp((k_s - \alpha_s)\Delta T)$$

Next, we consider a tumor reduction rate in asymmetric treatment case.

Lemma 2. *For asymmetric treatment (i.e., differential selective treatments), a tumor reduction rate after each round will decrease over time, i.e., $TR_k^{asym} > TR_{k+1}^{asym}$.*

We need to show $TR_k - TR_{k+1} > 0$ for asymmetric treatment. Tumor population can be calculated by solving Eq. (1) and the final inequality we need to prove is as follows: $x(t_{k+1}^{off}) \cdot x(t_k^{on}) - x(t_k^{off}) \cdot x(t_{k+1}^{on}) > 0$ and then we simply have the following to prove:

$$(\exp(k_2 - \alpha_2) - \exp(k_1 - \alpha_1)) \cdot (\exp(2k_2 - \alpha_2) - \exp(2k_1 - \alpha_1)) > 0$$

By simplifying this, we need to show whether $(k_2 - \alpha_2 > k_1 - \alpha_1) \cdot (2k_2 - \alpha_2 > 2k_1 - \alpha_1)$ is true. We will prove this by contradiction.

Proof. (Suppose not) $(k_2 - \alpha_2 > k_1 - \alpha_1) \cdot (2k_2 - \alpha_2 > 2k_1 - \alpha_1)$ is false. Then we consider two cases: A) $k_2 - \alpha_2 > k_1 - \alpha_1$ and $2k_2 - \alpha_2 \leq 2k_1 - \alpha_1$ or B) $k_2 - \alpha_2 < k_1 - \alpha_1$ and $2k_2 - \alpha_2 \geq 2k_1 - \alpha_1$. Note that we do not have the equality condition ($k_2 - \alpha_2 = k_1 - \alpha_1$) as we consider asymmetric treatment case here.

From the boundary condition and constraint (i.e., the same initial overall tumor growth and tumor reduction for the first treatment), we have the following conditions:

$$x_1(\Delta T) + x_2(\Delta T) = x_1(0)\exp(k_1\Delta T) + x_2(0)\exp(k_2\Delta T)$$
$$= (x_1(0) + x_2(0))\exp(k_s\Delta T)$$
$$x_1(t_1^{off}) + x_2(t_1^{off}) = x_1(\Delta T)\exp((k_1 - \alpha_1)\Delta T) + x_2(\Delta T)\exp((k_2 - \alpha_2)\Delta T)$$
$$= (x_1(\Delta T) + x_2(\Delta T))\exp((k_s - \alpha_s)\Delta T)$$

where the first equation represents the same initial tumor burden and the second equation represents the same initial efficacy. If we rearrange and use compositions (i.e., divided by the total population) and divided by $\exp(\Delta T)$):

$$p_1^0\exp(2k_1 - \alpha_1) + p_2^0\exp(2k_2 - \alpha_2) = \exp(2k_s - \alpha_s)$$
$$= p_1^0\exp(k_1 + k_s - \alpha_s) + p_2^0\exp(k_2 + k_s - \alpha_s)$$

where $p_i^0 = \frac{x_i(0)}{x_1(0)+x_2(0)}$, $\sum_i p_i^0 = 1$ and we have the following:

$$p_1^0(\exp(2k_1 - \alpha_1) - \exp(k_1 + k_s - \alpha_s)) = p_2^0(\exp(k_2 + k_s - \alpha_s) - \exp(2k_2 - \alpha_2))$$

Then, we have two cases: 1) $2k_1 - \alpha_1 > k_1 + k_s - \alpha_s$ and $k_2 + k_s - \alpha_s > 2k_2 - \alpha_2$ or 2) $2k_1 - \alpha_1 < k_1 + k_s - \alpha_s$ and $k_2 + k_s - \alpha_s < 2k_2 - \alpha_2$. Note that we consider asymmetric condition and thus do not consider when the equation is equal to zero since it results in $k_1 - \alpha_1 = k_s - \alpha_s = k_2 - \alpha_2$. Then we simply have the followings:

$$\begin{cases} k_1 - \alpha_1 < k_s - \alpha_s < k_2 - \alpha_2 \text{ for case A)} \\ k_1 - \alpha_1 > k_s - \alpha_s > k_2 - \alpha_2 \text{ for case B)} \end{cases}$$

Also, we have

$$\exp(2k_s - \alpha_s) = p_1^0 \exp(2k_s - \alpha_s) + p_2^0 \exp(2k_s - \alpha_s)$$
$$= p_1^0 \exp(k_1 + k_s - \alpha_s) + p_2^0 \exp(k_1 + k_s - \alpha_s)$$

Since this should hold in general (i.e., for any (p_1^0, p_2^0)), we could consider the case where $k_1 = k_s = k_2$. Then, it is simple to show contradiction from the assumption, for instance, for case A), $2k_2 - \alpha_2 > 2k_1 - \alpha_1$ (contradiction, $\because$ $2k_2 - \alpha_2 \leq 2k_1 - \alpha_1$). Similarly, for case B), $2k_1 - \alpha_1 > 2k_2 - \alpha_2$ (contradiction, $\because 2k_2 - \alpha_2 \geq 2k_1 - \alpha_1$).

We consider the rate of change in tumor sensitivity (or rate of tumor adaptation) by taking the slope of the percent tumor reduction values for successive doses. In other words, the greater the decrease in tumor reduction, the more negative the rate of change in tumor sensitivity. We can define a rate of tumor adaptation, which refers to how quickly the population of composition changes, by taking the absolute value of this metric [9].

Definition 2. *A rate of tumor adaption (TA) is defined as follows:*

$$TA_k \triangleq \frac{|TR_{k+1} - TR_k|}{\Delta T} \tag{5}$$

where TR_k and TR_{k+1} represent tumor reduction at the kth and $(k+1)^{th}$ round of treatment.

Based on Lemma 1, this value for symmetric treatment is equal to zero. On the other hand, for asymmetric treatment regime, TR_{k+1}^{asym} is smaller than TR_k^{asym} and thus a rate of tumor adaptation increases; From Lemma 2, since TR_k^{asym} is always greater than TR_{k+1}^{asym}, the greater the difference between TR_k^{asym} and TR_{k+1}^{asym}, the value of tumor adaptation rate increases and thus the effectiveness of drug killing decreases.

Lemma 3. *For symmetric treatment, a rate of tumor adaptation is zero but for asymmetric treatment, a rate of tumor adaption is positive (i.e., tumor reduction decreases for successive doses).*

Proof. by Definition 2 and Lemma 1 and 2.

Theorem 1. *With the same initial overall tumor size at the time of treatment and the same initial efficacy on the overall tumor, differential-imposed selective pressures on the individual sub-populations (i.e., asymmetric treatment) results in higher tumor burden in the long-term compared to symmetric treatment.*

Proof. $TR_1^{sym} = TR_1^{asym}$ by assumption (i.e., the same initial efficacy on the overall tumor) and Lemma 3 (i.e., a tumor reduction rate is constant in symmetric treatment but decreases over time in asymmetric treatment).

Thus, in the case where two different regimes (i.e., symmetric and asymmetric treatment) have the same initial efficacy on the overall tumor, differential selective pressures on the individual sub-populations lead to different drug sensitivities and result in long-term therapeutic outcome. Now the question is how we could use such results to design treatment strategy for controlling such system. To address this, we consider differential selective pressures as a factor of the cost function in the following section.

4   Differential Selective Pressures as a Factor of the Cost Function

Motivated by the effects of distinct drug selective pressures on long-term tumor response, we consider how to use this principled concept in treatment design that ultimately minimize relapse. In this section, we formulate an optimal control problem to enable better design of therapeutics by considering differential selective pressures as a factor of the cost function.

We consider a general form

$$\dot{N}_i(t) = (k_i - \alpha_i d)N_i(t), \ i = \{1, \cdots, m\} \tag{6}$$

where N_i represents the population of the i-th cell type. Then, we define a composition rate:

$$p_i(t) = \frac{N_i(t)}{\sum_{j=1}^{m} N_j(t)} = \frac{N_i(t)}{N_T(t)} \tag{7}$$

where $N_T(t) = \sum_{j=1}^{m} N_j(t)$. The rate of composition change is as follows:

$$\dot{p}_i(t) = \frac{\dot{N}_i(t)N_T(t) - N_i(t)\dot{N}_T(t)}{N_T(t)^2} = \frac{\dot{N}_i(t)}{N_T(t)} - p_i(t)\frac{\dot{N}_T(t)}{N_T(t)}$$

$$= (k_i - \alpha_i d - \sum_{j=1}^{m}(k_j - \alpha_j d) \cdot p_j(t)) \cdot p_i(t)$$

Lemma 4. *For symmetric treatment, sub-population composition does not change over time.*

Proof. For symmetric treatment, we have $k_i - \alpha_i d = k_j - \alpha_j d$ where $i \neq j$.

$$\dot{p}_i(t) = \left(k_i - \alpha_i d - (k_i - \alpha_i d) \cdot (\sum_{j=1}^{m} p_j(t))\right)p_i(t)$$

$$= (k_i - \alpha_i d - (k_i - \alpha_i d) \cdot 1) \cdot p_i(t) = 0$$

Thus, symmetric treatment condition guarantees $\dot{p}_i(t) = 0 \ \forall i$ (i.e., sufficient condition). To show that it is a necessary condition for $\dot{p}_i(t) = 0 \ \forall i$, we consider the following lemma:

Lemma 5. *If the following holds:* $\forall i$, *if* $k_i - \alpha_i d - \sum_{j=1}^m (k_j - \alpha_j d) \cdot p_j(t) = 0$
(i.e., $\dot{p}_i(t) = 0$*), then* $k_i - \alpha_i d = k_j - \alpha_j d$ *where* $i \neq j$*).*

Proof. (by induction)
Assuming that it is true for m, i.e., $\forall i = \{1, \cdots m\}$, $k_i - \alpha_i d - \sum_{j=1}^m (k_j - \alpha_j d) \cdot p_j(t) = 0$ implies $k_i - \alpha_i d = k_j - \alpha_j d$ where $i \neq j$. Then, we prove that it is true for $m + 1$:

$$k_i - \alpha_i d - \sum_{j=1}^{m+1} (k_j - \alpha_j d) \cdot p_j(t) = 0$$

Rearranging this equation:

$$(k_i - \alpha_i d)(\sum_{j=1, j \neq i}^{m+1} p_j(t)) = \sum_{j=1, j \neq i}^{m+1} (k_j - \alpha_j d)\dot{p}_j(t)$$

Using the assumption that $(k_i - \alpha_i d) \cdot (\sum_{j=1, j \neq i}^m p_j(t)) = \sum_{j=1, j \neq i}^m (k_j - \alpha_j d) \cdot p_j(t)$ implies $k_i - \alpha_i d = k_j - \alpha_j d$ where $i \neq j$ and $i = \{1, \cdots, m\}$. Then, we have

$$(k_i - \alpha_i d) \cdot p_{m+1}(t) = (k_{m+1} - \alpha_{m+1}d) \cdot p_{m+1}(t)$$

where $i \neq m + 1$ and thus $k_i - \alpha_i d = k_{m+1} - \alpha_{m+1}d$.

Theorem 2. *To avoid increasing rate of tumor adaptation, we need to satisfy* $\forall i, (k_i - \alpha_i d) = (k_j - \alpha_j d)$ *where* $i \neq j$*, i.e., conserve sub-population composition over time.*

Proof. by Lemma 4, 5 and Theorem 1.

Now we define the objective function in the following form:

$$J(\alpha) = rN(T) + \int_0^T \{qN(t) + s\alpha(t)\}dt \tag{8}$$

$$= \sum_{i=1}^m r_i N_i(T) + \int_0^T \{\sum_{i=1}^n q_i N_i(t) + \sum_{j=1}^m s_j \alpha_j(t)\}dt$$

In this equation r_i, q_i and s_j denote weighting factors of total population, population during treatment and control effort respectively. Then the optimization problem can be described with the constraints $k_i - \alpha_i d = k_j - \alpha_j d$ for all i where $i \neq j$ to avoid increasing rate of tumor adaptation and thus ultimately minimize tumor burden in the long term:

$$\min J(\alpha, u)$$
$$\text{s.t.} \quad \dot{N}_i(t) = (k_i - \alpha_i d)N_i(t)$$
$$k_i - \alpha_i d = u, \quad \forall i$$
$$0 \leq \alpha_i \leq \alpha_{max} \tag{9}$$

where we also consider the maximum drug effect (α_{max}) as inequality conditions. By solving the optimization problem, we minimize the overall tumor burden while maintaining sub-population composition in order to minimize tumor adaptation.

5 Numerical Simulation Results and Discussion

In this section, we consider numerical simulations to demonstrate the effects of drug selective pressure by solving the optimization problem. To demonstrate this, we consider the system of equations (1) and solve optimization problem using Lagrangian method:

$$J(\alpha, u) = rN(T) + \int_0^T \{qN(t) + s\alpha(t)\}dt + \sum_{i=1}^m \mu_i(k_i - \alpha_i - u)^2$$

$$+ \sum_{i=1}^m l_i S_i(\alpha_i - \alpha_{max})^2 + \sum_{i=1}^m b_i V_i(\alpha_i)^2$$

where μ_i, l_i, b_i represent Lagrangian multiplier for equality condition and inequality condition respectively. Here $S_i = 1$ if $\alpha_i - \alpha_{max} > 0$ and $S_i = 0$ if $\alpha_i - \alpha_{max} \leq 0$. Similarly $V_i = 1$ if $\alpha_i < 0$ and $V_i = 0$ if $\alpha_i \geq 0$. In a simple two-population model, the objective function is as follows:

$$J(\alpha, u) = r_1 x_1(T) + r_2 x_2(T) + \int_0^T \{q_1 x_1(t) + q_2 x_2(t) + s_1 \alpha_1(t) + s_2 \alpha_2(t)\}dt$$

$$+ \mu_1(k_1 - \alpha_1 - u)^2 + \mu_2(k_2 - \alpha_2 - u)^2$$

$$+ l_1 \cdot S_1(\alpha_1 - \alpha_{max})^2 + l_2 \cdot S_2(\alpha_2 - \alpha_{max})^2 + b_1 \cdot V_1(\alpha_1)^2 + b_2 \cdot V_2(\alpha_2)^2$$

Herein, we consider optimization variable α_1 as constant value for the simplicity. By increasing Lagrangian multipliers, equality and inequality conditions hold. In simulation study, we consider optimization problems with and without the equality constraint to demonstrate how penalizing different selective pressures affects tumor adaptation, sub-population composition changes and long term effect of treatment. We consider three different scenarios: 1) the same initial sub-populations with the same growth rate, 2) different initial sub-populations with the same growth rate, and 3) the same initial sub-populations with different growth rates.

Figure 2 (left) shows the first scenario with and without penalizing different selective pressures. The parameters in this case are as follows: $x_1(0) = x_2(0) = 0.5$, $k_s = k_1 = k_2 = 0.1$, $\Delta T = 4$, $\alpha_s = 0.22$, $\alpha_{max} = 1$ and α_2 is obtained using Eq. (3) for no constraint case. Total tumor burden without constraint is higher than total tumor burden with constraint; In Fig. 2 (left-top), the red line shows the total population dynamics without considering constraint and we observe that sub-population composition changes over multiple rounds of drug treatment as shown in Fig. 2 (left-middle, bottom) and tumor reduction decreases after each round of treatment as shown in Fig. 2 (right-bottom). On the other hand, by conserving sub-population composition or rate of tumor adaptation, total tumor burden decreases more as shown in Fig. 2 (top) and tumor reduction does not change over time in successive drug treatment as shown in Fig. 2 (right-top). Note that sub-population ratio is conserved over time as shown in Fig. 2 (bottom) and thus tumor adaptation is zero.

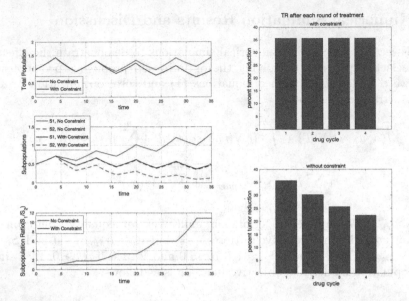

Fig. 2. Simulation result when the initial condition and growth rates are the same for both sub-populations. (Left) Top figure shows the overall tumor population dynamics, middle figure shows sub-population dynamics and bottom figure shows sub-population ratio $(\max(s_1, s_2)/\min(s_1, s_2))$. (Right) Tumor reduction (TR) rate after each round of treatment where TR is constant over time when tumor adaptation rate is considered in the objective function (top) and TR decreases over time when the tumor adaptation rate is not considered in the cost function (bottom).

Two additional simulation studies were performed to see different initial sub-population condition and the effect of different growth rate. Figure 3 (left) shows the effect of different initial sub-population conditions. All the parameters are the same as the previous case except the initial condition $x_1(0) = 0.65$ and $x_2(0) = 0.35$. Total tumor burden decreases more with constraint as shown in Fig. 3 (left-top) and sub-population ratio does not change over time as shown in Fig. 3 (left-bottom).

Figure 3 (right) shows the case with different growth rate ($k_s = 0.09$, $k_1 = 0.11$) where k_2 is obtained by using equation (2). Total tumor burden decreases more by penalizing differential selective pressure as shown in Fig. 3 (right-top). Note that sub-population composition does not change when drug treatment is applied to the system but when drug is off, sub-population composition changes due to the different growth rates as shown in Fig. 3 (right-bottom) due to the different growth rates.

Throughout numerical simulation studies, we demonstrated that the constraint in the optimization problem enables to penalize different selective pressures and thus reduce the tumor burden by reducing long-term drug resistance or tumor adaptation.

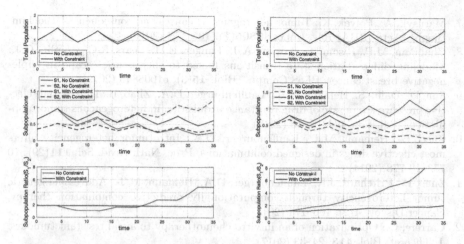

Fig. 3. Simulation result with different initial sub-population condition (left) and different growth rate (right). In each figure, top figure shows the overall tumor population dynamics, middle figure shows sub-population dynamics and bottom figure shows sub-population ratio.

6 Conclusion

In this paper, we consider tumor heterogeneity and selective pressure on sub-populations in the treatment design. By conserving sub-populations, we minimize tumor adaptation and thus reduce the long-term tumor burden. In future work, we will consider a more general form instead of using a simple two-population model to take mutations or cross-talk between each population into account which might decrease drug efficacy.

Acknowledgement. This work was supported in part by the National Cancer Institute (U54CA209988).

References

1. Matveev, A.S., Savkin, A.V.: Application of optimal control theory to analysis of cancer chemotherapy regimens. Syst. Control Lett. **46**(5), 311–321 (2002)
2. Oke, S.I., Matadi, M.B., Xulu, S.S.: Optimal control analysis of a mathematical model for breast cancer. Math. Comput. Appl. **23**(2), 21 (2018)
3. de Pillis, L.G., et al.: Chemotherapy for tumors: An analysis of the dynamics and a study of quadratic and linear optimal controls. Math. Biosci. **209**(1), 292–315 (2007)
4. Boldrini, J.L., Costa, M.I.: Therapy burden, drug resistance, and optimal treatment regimen for cancer chemotherapy. Math. Med. Biol. **17**(1), 33–51 (2000)
5. El-Sayes, N., Vito, A., Mossman, K.: Tumor heterogeneity: a great barrier in the age of cancer immunotherapy. Cancers **13**(4), 806 (2021)
6. Martelotto, L.G., Ng, C.K., Piscuoglio, S., Weigelt, B., Reis-Filho, J.S.: Breast cancer intra-tumor heterogeneity. Breast Cancer Res. **16**(3), 1–11 (2014)

7. Marusyk, A., Polyak, K.: Tumor heterogeneity: causes and consequences. Biochim. Biophy. Acta (BBA)-Rev. Cancer **1805**(1), 105–117 (2010)
8. Chapman, M.P., Risom, T., Aswani, A.J., Langer, E.M., Sears, R.C., Tomlin, C.J.: Modeling differentiation-state transitions linked to therapeutic escape in triple-negative breast cancer. PLoS Comput. Biol. **15**(3), e1006840 (2019)
9. Sun, D., Dalin, S., Hemann, M.T., Lauffenburger, D.A., Zhao, B.: Differential selective pressure alters rate of drug resistance acquisition in heterogeneous tumor populations. Sci. Rep. **6**(1), 1–13 (2016)
10. Zhao, B., Hemann, M.T., Lauffenburger, D.A.: Intratumor heterogeneity alters most effective drugs in designed combinations. Proc. Natl. Acad. Sci. **111**(29), 10 773–10 778 (2014)
11. Zhao, B., Pritchard, J.R., Lauffenburger, D.A., Hemann, M.T.: Addressing genetic tumor heterogeneity through computationally predictive combination therapy. Cancer Discov. **4**(2), 166–174 (2014)
12. Carrère, C.: Optimization of an in vitro chemotherapy to avoid resistant tumours. J. Theoret. Biol. **413**, 24–33 (2017)
13. Ledzewicz, U., Wang, S., Schättler, H., André, N., Heng, M.A., Pasquier, E.: On drug resistance and metronomic chemotherapy: a mathematical modeling and optimal control approach. Math. Biosci. Eng. **14**(1), 217 (2017)

Mathematical Modeling for Cancer Research

Improved Geometric Configuration for the Bladder Cancer BCG-Based Immunotherapy Treatment Model

Teddy Lazebnik[1]($\boxtimes$) and Svetlana Bunimovich-Mendrazitsky[2]

[1] Department of Cancer Biology, Cancer Institute, University College, London, UK
t.lazebnik@ucl.ac.uk
[2] Department of Mathematics, Ariel University, Ariel, Israel

Abstract. Bacillus Calmette–Guérin (BCG) immunotherapy has shown significant success for bladder cancer treatment, but due to the lack of personalization, it does not fulfill its full promise as the interaction between immunity and cancer varies significantly between patients and results in extremely different clinical outcomes. As personalized treatment developed, it is important to take into consideration the geometrical configuration of the bladder in order to get realistic results using spatio-temporal treatment models.

We present an extension to the model proposed by Lazebnik et al. [9] by improving the approximation of the bladder's geometry from sphere-ring to ellipsoid-ring [8]. We show the differences between the models on the clinical results and their influence on the optimal treatment protocol.

Keywords: Nonlinear systems · PDE cancer treatment model · Geometrical pde systems dynamics

1 Introduction and Related Work

Bladder cancer (BC) is a major clinical problem with an estimated 549,000 new cases and 200,000 deaths each year which makes it the 10th most common form of cancer worldwide [2]. Most of the incidents occur in developed and industrialized areas, such as Australia, North America, and Europe [2]. The high rates of recurrence, invasive surveillance strategies, and high treatment costs combine to make BC the single most expensive cancer in both the United States and England [3].

Treatment of non-invasive BC has not advanced significantly over the past five decades following the treatment protocol suggested by Morales et al. (1976) that involves weekly instillations of Bacillus Calmette–Guérin (BCG) [11]. The most common protocol is based upon treatment suggested by Morales et al. (1976) and involves weekly instillations of BCG over a 6-week period. It is called *induction treatment* protocol. BCG is a type of immunotherapy used to treat non-invasive BC [7]. The BCG treatment protocol has yet to be specifically optimized for those patients who do not achieve remission from the treatment that follows the current standard protocol.

© Springer Nature Switzerland AG 2021
G. Bebis et al. (Eds.): ISMCO 2021, LNBI 13060, pp. 63–67, 2021.
https://doi.org/10.1007/978-3-030-91241-3_6

Mathematical modeling is shown to be a useful tool in clinical settings in general and oncology in particular, allowing to investigate both the disease and possible treatments [1]. Several attempts were made to describe the cell dynamics taking into account biological interactions in the physical space based on partial differential equations (PDE) [4,9,10]. Specifically, the authors of [9] combined and extended the models proposed by [6,10] and shows how to evaluate the patient's spatial data - distribution of cancer polyps, to obtain a personalized treatment. However, [9] approximate the bladder's geometry using sphere-ring which may result in large errors due to the poor approximation of the bladder's geometry [8].

Based on the model by [9], we approximate the bladder's geometry using ellipsoid-ring configuration to obtain a more clinically accurate treatment protocol. The manuscript is organized as follows. First, we describe the model with the new geometrical configuration and the numerical methods used to solve it. Second, we obtain the treatment protocols based on the proposed model. Third, we compare the results of both models with clinical data. Finally, we discuss the improvements and limitations of the proposed model.

2   Mathematical Modeling Extension

2.1   Model Definition

We assume the bladder's geometry satisfies Eq. (1) as an approximation to the bladder's geometrical configuration:

$$r_0 \leq \frac{x^2}{g_1} + \frac{y^2}{g_2} + \frac{z^2}{g_3} \leq R. \tag{1}$$

In Eq. (1), the variables x, y, z are the Cartesian coordinate system, $r_0 = r_0^1 + r_0^2$ and $R = R^1 + R^2$ are the radius of the internal and external ellipsoids of the geometrical configuration, respectively. The bladder's geometry is approximated using a perfect (e.g., the parameters g_1, g_2, and g_3 are equal for the inner and outer ellipsoid) ellipsoid-ring while the real human bladder has additional three tunnels [6]. The geometry of the system and the transformation from the original (sphere-ring) approximation are visualized in Fig. 1.

2.2   Numerical Solution

All the numerical calculations have been performed with $C\#$ programming language (version 8.0) using an agent-based approach [5]. First, we sampled the space (Eq. (1)) using a polar coordinate system (ϕ, θ, r) such that the volume between each eight neighbor points is approximately the same. Second, each such segment is considered a "cell" and allocated to a state according to the initial and boundary condition of the system. At each point at time t, Eqs. (1–9) in [9] solved using the finite difference method where the state at time $t - 1$ is stored in the simulation memory while the spatial (diffusion) dynamics simulated using the particle-particle potentials method [13].

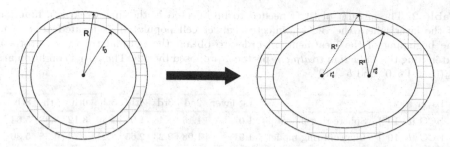

Fig. 1. Schematic view of the transformation between the model's geometry from [9] to the proposed one as shown in Eq. (1).

2.3 Treatment Protocol Based on Initial Tumor Distribution

Using the new geometrical configuration (see Sect. 2.1) and numerical analysis method (see Sect. 2.2) we take advantage of the treatment personalization method proposed by [9].

To carry out the numerical simulations of the tumor-immune model (Eqs. (1–10) in [9] and Eq. (1)), we used the parameter values from Table 3 in [9]. The results are shown in Table 1, where RP (Range of successful Protocols) is defined as the difference between the amount of BCG-uninfected cancer cell the most aggressive (largest b) and most non-aggressive treatment (lowest b) such that the treatment successed. In addition, AP (Average successful Protocol) is defined as the average BCG-uninfected cancer population size for all the possible combinations of different treatment protocols that differ in the distribution of the BCG-uninfected cancer cells in the layers of the urothelium such that the treatment will be successful. Namely, RP defines the range of successful treatments while AP defines the average of this set in the terms of BCG injection b as a function of the initial tumor cell distribution in the bladder's geometry. The treatment duration t_{max} is set to 42 days. In addition, parameters g_1, g_2, and g_3 (in Eq. (1)) set to $1.2, 1.35$, and 1, respectively [8]. Furthermore, the optimal treatment protocol in the manner of BCG injection b as a function of the layer of the urothelium the BCG-uninfected cancer cells are allocated at the beginning of the treatment, divided by the geometrical configuration used to approximate the bladder's geometry, is shown in Table 2.

Table 1. The sensitivity of the model to the initial distribution of cancer cells in different layers of the bladder at the beginning of treatment (t_0). The values were calculated over the first four weeks of the treatment [9].

Metric	Model	1 layer	2 layers	3 layers	4 layers	5 layers	6 layers
RP $[m^3 t \cdot 10^7]$	Sphere-ring [9]	1.90	1.63	1.36	0.88	0.70	0.54
RP $[m^3 t \cdot 10^7]$	Ellipsoid-ring	1.846	1.651	1.421	1.009	0.776	0.522
AP $[m^3 t \cdot 10^9]$	Sphere-ring [9]	1.157	1.155	1.159	1.158	1.159	1.157
AP $[m^3 t \cdot 10^9]$	Ellipsoid-ring	2.09	2.085	2.089	2.083	2.077	2.065

Table 2. The amount of BCG needed to be injected in the first week as a function of the layer where the BCG-uninfected cancer cell population is located at, during the beginning of the treatment, in order to obtain the optimal treatment protocol extendting the *induction treatment* protocol proposed by [12]. The initial condition are $T_u(0) = 1 \cdot 10^6$ and $b = 10^6$.

Layer	1st layer	2nd	3rd	4th	5th	6th	7th	8th
BCG ($b \cdot 10^6$) - Sphere-ring model [9]	1.07	1.16	1.48	1.91	2.49	3.12	3.88	5.04
BCG ($b \cdot 10^6$) - Ellipsoid-ring model	1.91	1.98	2.23	2.65	3.21	3.76	4.38	5.36

3   Discussion

In this research, we have proposed a better approximation of the human bladder in an ellipsoidal-ring to improve individualized BCG immunotherapy treatment. By comparing the results that based on the sphere-ring, the novel results show that in order to optimally use the *induction treatment* protocol after the first week, one would require almost twice the amount of BCG compared to the amount predicted by [9] in the case the cancer cells are located at the most shallow layer of the urothelium and the difference decreases as the initial layer the cells are located at is deeper, as shown in Table 2. This means, that the models highly differ for stages I and II in cancer where it is still in the shallow layers while converge where the diseases approach to stage III where the treatment is shown to be ineffective anyway [12].

In addition, one can notice that both models agree on the difference between the worst and the best treatment, as shown in Table 1 - the *RP* parameter. In addition, from the *AP* parameter in Table 1, it is shown that the average treatment successful protocol that differs in the distribution of the BCG-uninfected cancer cells in the layers of the urothelium are 80% higher in the case of the ellipsoid-ring compared to the sphere-ring which indicates that while the range of the treatment protocols is more or less equal, the average treatment in the ellipsoid-ring configuration should be much more aggressive to obtain a similar clinical outcome.

These results are evaluated for a mean case (patient) in the population and can be highly altered between patients according, but not limited, to their age, gender, and weight. One can overcome this challenge by introducing these parameters to the proposed model in one of two ways. One way is by setting personalized r_0 and R values in Eq. (1) according to a measurement of a single patent and recomputing the simulations results. A more generic way is to use machine learning methods to learn a regression model between these parameters and the r_0 and R parameters using a dataset of samples from a heterogeneous population of individuals (not necessarily patients). Once such a model is obtained, it can be used to extend the proposed model into a family of models, each one approximating a possible single patents' parameters.

The lack of recorded and publicly available clinical data regarding the course of bladder cancer BCG treatment, especially in the context of the BCG and cancer cells distribution in the bladder's geometry, results in the incapability of evaluating the presented outcomes in realistic settings. As more such data will become available, better parameter estimation and evaluation of the models are recommended. In addition, another possible future to further improve the accuracy of the model is to take into consideration the change over time of the geometrical configuration as the bladder fill and empty during the day.

References

1. Bhattacharya, S., Sah, P.P., Banerjee, A., Ray, S.: Structural impact due to PPQEE deletion in multiple cancer associated protein - integrin V: an in silico exploration. Biosystems **98**, 104216 (2020)
2. Bray, F., Ferlay, J., Soerjomataram, I., Siegel, R.L., Torre, L., Jemal, A.: Global cancer statistics 2018: Globocan estimates of incidence and mortality worldwide for 36 cancers in 185 countries. CA Cancer J. Cling. **68**(2), 394–424 (2018)
3. Eylert, M., et al.: Falling bladder cancer incidence from 1990 to 2009 is not producing universal mortality improvements. J. Clin. Urol. **7**(2), 90–98 (2014)
4. Fridman, A., Kao, C.: Mathematical modeling of biological processs. Lecture Notes on Mathematical Modeling in the Life Sciences (2014)
5. Fullstone, G., Wood, J., Holcombe, M., Battaglia, G.: Modelling the transport of nanoparticles under blood flow using an agent-based approach. Sci. Rep. **5**, 10649 (2015)
6. Guzev, E., Halachmi, S., Bunimovich-Mendrazitsky, S.: Additional extension of the mathematical model for BCG immunotherapy of bladder cancer and its validation by auxiliary tools. Int. J. Nonlinear Sci. Num.l Simul. **20**, 675–689 (2019)
7. Herr, H.W., et al.: Bacillus calmette-Guérin therapy alters the progression of superficial bladder cancer. J. Clin. Oncol. **6**, 1450–1455 (1988)
8. Kristiansen, N.K., Ringgaard, S., Nygaard, H., Djurhuus, J.C.: Effect of bladder volume, gender and body position on the shape and position of the urinary bladder. Scand. J. Urol. Nephrol. **38**, 462–468 (2004)
9. Lazebnik, T., Bunimovich-Mendrazitsky, S., Haroni, N.: PDE based geometry model for BCG immunotherapy of bladder cancer. Biosystems **200**, 104319 (2021)
10. Lazebnik, T., Yanetz, S., Bunimovich-Mendrazitsky, S., Haroni, N.: Treatment of bladder cancer using BCG immunotherapy: PDE modeling. Partial Diff. Equ. **26**, 203–219 (2020)
11. Morales, A., Eidinger, D., Bruce, A.: Intracavity Bacillus Calmette-Guérin in the treatment of superficial bladder tumors. J. Urol. **116**, 180–183 (1976)
12. Paterson, D., Patel, A.: Bactillus Calmette-Guerin (BCG) immunotherapy for bladder cancer: review of complications and their treatment. Aust. NZJ Surg. **68**, 340–344 (1998)
13. Schöneberg, J., Ullrich, A., Noé, F.: Simulation tools for particle-based reaction-diffusion dynamics in continuous space. BMC Biophys 7(11) (2014)

Computational Methods for Anticancer Drug Development

Run for Your Life – An Integrated Virtual Tissue Platform for Incorporating Exercise Oncology into Immunotherapy

Josua Aponte-Serrano[✉] and Amit Hagar

Intelligent Systems Engineering, School of Informatics, Computing and Engineering, Indiana University—Bloomington, Bloomington, IN 47405, USA
joaponte@iu.edu

Abstract. The purpose of this paper is to introduce a novel *in silico* platform for simulating early stage solid tumor growth and anti-tumor immune response. We present the model, test the sensitivity and robustness of its parameters, and calibrate it with clinical data from exercise oncology experiments which offer a natural biological backdrop for modulation of anti-tumor immune response. We then perform a virtual experiment with the model that demonstrate its usefulness in guiding pre-clinical and clinical studies of immunotherapy. The virtual experiment shows how dosage and/or frequency of immunotherapy drugs can be optimized based on the aerobic fitness of the patient, so that possible adverse side effects of the treatment can be minimized.

Keywords: Cancer modeling · Immunotherapy · CompuCell3D

1 Introduction

Computational modeling is playing increasingly important roles in advancing a system-level mechanistic understanding of complex interrelated biological processes. Here we present a computational platform that can interrogate potential mechanisms underlying the effect of aerobic fitness on anti-tumor immune response. These effects, documented in pre-clinical [1] and clinical studies [2] support the inclusion of aerobic fitness as a biological variable in clinical contexts. This platform can contribute to the personalization of immunotherapy by optimizing dosage and frequency of treatment and by reducing the risk other adverse side effects [3].

Our basics assumption is that aerobic fitness acts as a tumor suppressor through a systemic enhancement of anti-tumor immune response. This systemic effect is a result of metabolic and endocrinal modifications, which can be modulated with exercise training. While the exact mechanisms behind this effect are currently under investigation, documented pre-clinical experiments point at two potential candidates: (1) increased trafficking of NK cells into the TME [4] and (2) hypoxia-tolerant suppression of the recruitment of immune inhibitory cells (CD4$^+$FOXP3$^+$ Tregs) [5]. The model presented here focuses on the latter mechanism.

© Springer Nature Switzerland AG 2021
G. Bebis et al. (Eds.): ISMCO 2021, LNBI 13060, pp. 71–77, 2021.
https://doi.org/10.1007/978-3-030-91241-3_7

2 Methods

2.1 Model Description

The model is a spatiotemporal representation of a TME of a solid tumor in its early stages (T0 to T1). Tumor cells adopt four different phenotypes: "oxphos" (relying on oxidative phosphorylation), "glycolytic" (elevated glycolysis when the surrounding tissue becomes hypoxic), "necrotic" and "apoptotic". Tumor cells grow, divide and invade their environment. The growth rate of tumor cells is limited by the availability of oxygen (modeled as a field) which cells consume from the environment. The fitness parameter controls the oxygen level at which cell transition metabolic phenotype: as oxygen gets depleted, tumor cells change from "oxphos" to "glycolytic". When oxygen is severely depleted, glycolytic cells become necrotic and die. Glycolytic cells secrete lactate (modeled also as a field) to the TME. Lactate serves as a recruiting signal for the tumor promoter cells.

Our model includes two types of immune cells: CD8$^+$ Lymphocytes tumor suppressors ("CTLs") and CD4$^+$FOXP3$^+$ tumor promoters ("Tregs"). CTLs are constantly recruited to the tumor site and induce apoptosis in the tumor cells they come into contact with. Upon contact with tumor cells, tumor suppressors also release a IFNγ cytokine signal (modeled as a field) attracting other CTLs. The acidification of the TME by the glycolytic cells results in recruitment of Tregs to the tumor site. Recruited Tregs move through the tissue to areas of higher concentration of lactate. "Tregs" inhibit the "CTLs" they come in close proximity to. This inhibition prevents "CTLs" from inducing apoptosis in cancer cells.

We implemented the model in CompuCell3D (CC3D), an open-source modeling environment that allows specification and simulation of multicellular models, diffusing fields and biochemical networks [6]. Diffusion solvers integrate partial differential equations describing the diffusion of oxygen, lactate and IFNγ across the whole simulation domain. Outcomes of the simulation are dependent on the parameter values associated with aerobic fitness and with the emergent patterns of TME invasion associated with availability of resources and immune response (Fig. 1).

2.2 Parameter Estimation and Calibration

Simulation parameters corresponding to the spatial properties of human solid tumor cells, transport of chemicals and rates of immune response were estimated from the literature. Our model is simulated over 10^{-6} lattice sites representing up to 5×10^4 individual cells. Each lattice site corresponds to 16 um such that the simulation domain represents a 16 mm^2 tissue cross section. We assumed that cancer cells occupy an area of 256 μm^2. When sufficient resources are available, tumor cells grow and divide every 24 h. Conversely, when resources are depleted cells die within 12 h, and when "CTLs" induce apoptosis, cells die within 8 h. We estimated the infiltration rates of "CTLs" (1 cell every 1.5 h) and "Tregs" (1 cell every 1 h) using intramural density data, showing that the "CTL"/"Treg" ratio is 5:1 [7]. The intrinsic random motility and the contact energy were fixed so that tumor cells can detach from each other and invade the surrounding tissue [4]. We assumed that the homeostatic concentration of oxygen in tissue is 4.3 ×

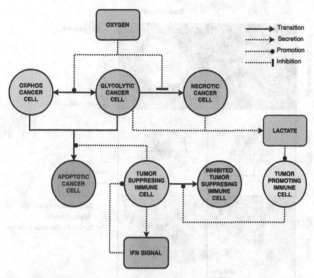

Fig. 1. The model simulates the early stage of solid tumor progression from which a growth rate can be calculated. Tumor cells grow in the TME and become more glycolytic, in a rate that depends on the host's aerobic fitness and tolerance to hypoxia. Tumor cells die through apoptosis or necrosis (lack of oxygen or death by CTLs). CTLs and Tregs react to cytokine and lactate fields secreted by tumor cells. Tumor cells grow until they saturate the grid.

10^{-4} Mol/L [8]. Transport parameters were estimated from the literature. Aerobic fitness was defined as the oxygen concentration threshold at which tumor cells changed from "oxphos" to "glycolytic". We simulated virtual cohort of 200 virtual subjects divided into 10 aerobic fitness levels. Sensitivity analysis on the aerobic fitness parameter show upper and lower bounds below and above which the effects on tumor growth remain constant. To calibrate remaining parameters of the model we matched it to clinical results from breast cancer patients where an aerobic score metric was used [11].

3 Results

3.1 Model Reproduces Key Mechanisms of Immunoregulation by the TME

Immune Suppresors and Immune Promoters Dynamics
Clinical studies have shown that intratumoral CTLs/Treg ratio is a significant prognostic marker for cancer patients and pre-clinical studies have tied this marker to hypoxic conditions in the TME [8]. In our model we introduced two scales of immune cells trafficking (Fig. 2). The first is the seeding rate to the TME; the second is the movement within the TME, implemented with a chemotaxis mechanism. The seeding rates and densities were calibrated using data on respective densities from hot vs. cold tumors in humans [6]. "CTLs" migrate towards the "IFNγ" cytokine field, "Tregs" migrate towards the lactate field.

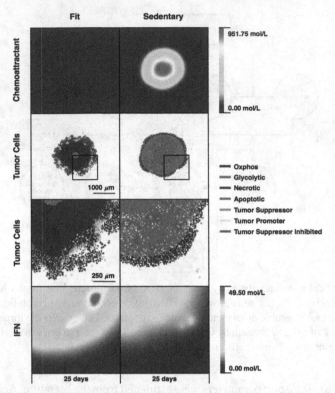

Fig. 2. The more aerobically fit is the host, the less glycolytic its tumor cells are relative to a sedentary host. Consequently, recruitment of Trges that can block CTLs is down regulated relative to a sedentary host, and tumor growth will be relatively suppressed. CTLs move towards the tumor along a cytokine gradient ("INFγ"). Tregs move towards the tumor along the lactate gradient that glycolytic tumor cells secrete. Once infiltrated into the TME, they can block the ability of nearby CTLs to kill tumor cells.

Effect of Aerobic Fitness on Tumor Progression Rate

We simulated a virtual cohort of 200 virtual subjects divided into 10 aerobic fitness levels. The model connects variations in fitness levels to variations in anti-tumor immune response and consequently to variations in tumor growth rates each of which yields a distinct tumor growth curve (Fig. 3A). A similar effect of suppression of tumor growth when inoculation followed endurance exercise was qualitatively demonstrated in pre-clinical studies [7]. The model behaves qualitatively in accordance with a similar plot of tumor doubling times vs. fitness levels from a pilot study in recently diagnosed T1 invasive ductal carcinoma patients (Fig. 3B, C).

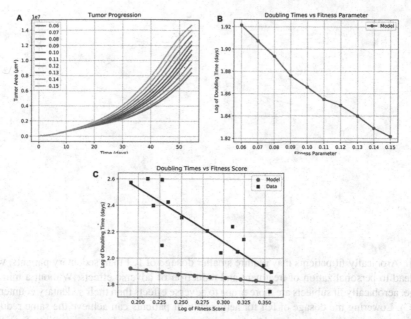

Fig. 3. The model was run on 200 virtual subjects, divided into equal size distinct aerobic fitness levels. Each fitness level generated an average growth rate (3A). These average growth rates where then plotted against the fitness levels on a logarithmic scale (3B). The model behaves qualitatively in accordance with a similar plot of tumor doubling times vs. fitness levels from a pilot study in recently diagnosed T1 invasive ductal carcinoma patients (3C) [14].

3.2 Incorporating Aerobic Fitness into the Personalization of Immunotherapy

While showing remarkable success in patients, immunotherapy treatments can lead to autoimmune adverse effects such as myocarditis, pericardial diseases, and vasculitis [5]. Personalized dosing could mitigate adverse effects. Preclinical studies have shown that aerobically fit patients may require lower dosage of immune check inhibitors (ICI) than sedentary patients [10]. To test this hypothesis, we implemented ICI in our model as an increased efficacy of "CTLs" killing. Cytotoxicity was quantified as additional "IFNγ" cytokine [11]. Performing a virtual experiment on aerobically fit and sedentary virtual subjects treated with ICI, simulations show that without a mitigated dosage, aerobically fit subjects are more prone to adverse effects than their sedentary counterparts (Fig. 4A, B). Lowering the ICI dosage for aerobically fit patients can achieve the same reduction of tumor growth relative to their sedentary counterparts but with lower probability for adverse effects (Fig. 4C, D). In order to translate this result to a clinical setting (Fig. 4E, F). future studies should identify potential markers for aerobic fitness with which such personalization can be accomplished.

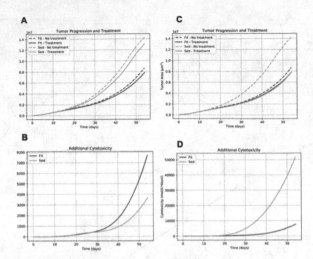

Fig. 4. Arobically fit patients may require smaller dosage of ICI than sedentary patients, which may lead to personalization of treatment and reduction of adverse effects. Without a mitigated dosage, aerobically fit subjects are more prone to adverse effects than their sedentary counterparts (4A, C). Lowering the dosage of ICI for aerobically fit patients can achieve the same reduction of tumor growth relative to their sedentary counterparts but with a lower probability for adverse effects (4B, D)

4 Discussion

We have shown how to generate a time series of TME snapshots during anti-tumor immune response, and how to personalize dosing of ICI for aerobically fit patients in order to lower the risk of adverse effects. In collaboration with cancer biologists and clinicians this platform can be used for improving *in vivo* experimental design and personalization of clinical outcomes.

The hypothesis that underlies the model presented here, connects exercise-induced increased hypoxia-tolerance to more efficient anti-tumor immune response, and requires chronic endurance training (CET) which can be achieved in pre-clinical exercise oncology with forced running wheels [12]. The idea here is that CET induces hypoxia tolerance in the skeletal muscles and in other tissues, and as a result, TMEs are more susceptible to the degradation of HIF1α [13]. This degradation is an upstream factor in a signaling cascade leading to increased anti-tumor immune efficiency, as HIF1α is known to recruit, via cytokine signaling, Trges into the tumor micro-environment, which suppress CTLs [7]. A pre-clinical study detected a twofold decrease in intratumoral Tregs/CTLs ratio in exercised mice relative to their sedentary counterparts [9].

Our platform can perform virtual experiments with no wet-lab or clinical costs, and is proposed here as tool for pre-clinical and clinical researchers. The tool is limited in several ways. First, to obtain simulation results in a reasonable time we must limit the computational cost. Consequently, our grid size is currently bounded by 5×10^{-4} cells. This size allows the simulation to be sensitive to spatiotemporal and stochastic features of the dynamics. Second, specific circumstances may require scaling up to 3D but for most clinical endpoints, a cross section of the TME may be a good approximation. Third, we introduced only two types of immune cells and three types of fields. From our experience, however, a direct dialogue between model developers and clinicians may help optimize the platform for each specific usage.

Our *in silico* platform is a safe playground for experimentation in dosage scheduling and frequency, as it can easily allow modulation of duration and timing of activation signaling to achieve the most effective treatment. Finally, our platform can easily incorporate and test combination of different types of immunotherapies with other standard-of-care therapies and probe potential synergistic effects. For example, since aerobic exercise promotes oxygenation, it can mimic the effects of antiangiogenic therapy, where different aerobic fitness levels can be calibrated to represent different dosage of such a therapy.

References

1. Ashcraft, K.A., Peace, R.M., Betof, A.S., Dewhirst, M.W., Jones, L.W.: Efficacy and mechanisms of aerobic exercise on cancer initiation, progression, and metastasis: a critical systematic review of in vivo preclinical data. Can. Res. **76**(14), 4032–4050 (2016). https://doi.org/10.1158/0008-5472.CAN-16-0887
2. Friedenreich, C.M.: Physical activity and breast cancer: review of the epidemiologic evidence and biologic mechanisms. In: Senn, H.-J., Otto, F. (eds.) Clinical Cancer Prevention, pp. 125–139. Springer, Heidelberg (2011). https://doi.org/10.1007/978-3-642-10858-7_11
3. Salem, J., et al.: Spectrum of cardiovascular toxicities of immune checkpoint inhibitors: a pharmacovigilance study. Lancet Oncol. **19**(12), 1579–1589 (2018). https://doi.org/10.1016/S1470-2045(18)30608-9
4. Pedersen, L., et al.: Voluntary running suppresses tumor growth through epinephrine- and IL-6-dependent NK cell mobilization and redistribution. Cell Metab. **23**, 1–9 (2016). https://doi.org/10.1016/j.cmet.2016.01.011
5. Hypoxia-driven immunosuppression: a new reason to use thermal therapy in the treatment of cancer. Int. J. Hyperth. **26**(3), 232–246. https://doi.org/10.3109/02656731003601745
6. Mendelsohn, J., et al.: The Molecular Basis of Cancer. Sounders, USA, p. 274 (2015)
7. Kather, J.N., et al.: Topography of cancer-associated immune cells in human solid tumors. Elife **7**, e36967 (2018). https://doi.org/10.7554/eLife.36967
8. Casciari, J.J., et al.: Variations in tumor cell growth rates and metabolism with oxygen concentration, glucose concentration, and extracellular pH. J. Cell. Physiol. **151**(2), 386–394 (1992)
9. Hagar, A., et al.: Endurance training slows breast tumor growth in mice by suppressing Treg cells recruitment to tumors. BMC Cancer **19**(1), 536 (2019). https://doi.org/10.1186/s12885-019-5745-7
10. Wennerberg, E., et al.: Exercise reduces immune suppression and breast cancer progression in a preclinical model. Oncotarget **11**(4), 452–461 (2020)
11. Postow, M.A., Sidlow, R., Hellmann, M.D.: Immune-related adverse events associated with immune checkpoint blockade. NEJM **378**(2), 158–168 (2018). https://doi.org/10.1056/NEJMra1703481
12. Melo, L., Hagar, A.: How to train a mouse. Am. J. Cancer Res. **9**(6), 1246–1253 (2019)
13. Petrova, V., Annicchiarico-Petruzzelli, M., Melino, G., Amelio, I.: The hypoxic tumour microenvironment. Oncogenesis **7**(1), 10 (2018). https://doi.org/10.1038/s41389-017-0011-9
14. Hagar, A., et al.: Muscular endurance and progression rates of early-stage invasive ductal carcinoma: a pilot study. Breast J. **24**(5), 849–851 (2018)

Author Index

Printed in the United States
by Baker & Taylor Publisher Services

Printed in the United States
by Baker & Taylor Publisher Services